It's a Long Way from Llano

JAMES G. TEER

It's a Long Way from Llano

THE JOURNEY OF A WILDLIFE BIOLOGIST

TEXAS A&M UNIVERSITY PRESS
COLLEGE STATION

This paper meets the requirements of ANSI/NISO Z39.48-1992
(Permanence of Paper).
Binding materials have been chosen for durability.

On title page: Canada goose on nest. Photo by Bob Klopman,
courtesy Delta Waterfowl Research Station, Delta, Manitoba.

Library of Congress Cataloging-in-Publication Data
Teer, James G.
It's a long way from Llano : the journey of a wildlife biologist / by
James G. Teer. — 1st ed.
p. cm.
Includes bibliographical references and index.
ISBN-13: 978-1-60344-068-4 (cloth : alk. paper)
ISBN-10: 1-60344-068-2 (cloth : alk. paper)
1. Teer, James G. 2. Biologists—Texas—Biography. 3. College teachers—Texas—
Biography. 4. Wildlife conservation—Texas. 5. Wildlife management—Texas.
I. Title. II. Title: Journey of a wildlife biologist.
QH31.T42A3 2008
639.9092—dc22
[B]
2008011033

THANK YOU FOR
SHOPPING AT THE
AAG STORE

24/2012 8:34AM   13
0004Z074   Kharra

11 Booklets $1.00
E ST $1.00
1              $0.00

NS   1Q
TOTAL $1.00
ASH $1.00
NE $0.00

CONTENTS

Jim Teer spent more than sixty years as a wildlife biologist employed by conservation agencies, universities, and foundations.

PREFACE

AT RETIREMENT, after a career spanning five decades and lasting through my eightieth birthday, I found myself yearning for the old times, when I was employed and engaged in wildlife conservation and management.

I was reasonably successful in my work and held responsible positions in state and federal organizations, nongovernmental agencies, and universities. After serving as head of the Department of Wildlife and Fisheries Sciences at Texas A&M University, I became the executive director of the Rob and Bessie Welder Wildlife Foundation and served in that role for more than twenty years. Over the years I was selected by our government and by international organizations to serve on task forces, committees, boards, and advisory groups to address issues in conservation science and education. As my career matured, I became involved in challenges beyond local and national scope, and international travel became part of my work. As a result, I was privileged to work in several regions of the world and gained more intimate understanding of conservation needs and issues at the global level.

To no longer participate in conservation affairs was difficult for me. Retirement came late by choice, and it presented some troubled times. I felt isolated, left out of meaningful activities and leadership roles that had heretofore been assigned to me. When these responsibilities ended, my self-worth was reduced. I have since learned that many retirees undergo a difficult withdrawal, often longing to return to their former activities.

Such feelings are not universal; some wish to get as far away from their former work as they can. But in my experience, this is rarely true of wildlife biologists, who seem to develop a mission and commitment to the natural world from which they cannot escape. More than a few continue to hunt, fish, and volunteer for conservation interests.

Conservation was the center of my life, but it was not the source of my identity. I grew up in a culture of hunting and fishing. As an adult, I saw no dichotomy between protecting and utilizing the natural world. The two were one and the same in the practice of conservation and natural resource management, serving the needs of both wildlife and people.

In retirement, I missed the people who had been my colleagues and companions. I felt loss for those who died and anxiety for those left in advanced age. A sense of futility found an uncomfortable place in me. Death seemed a terrible waste of lifetimes of talent, wisdom, beauty, understanding, and joy. I also began to feel that the results of some of these lives should be collected and preserved.

I knew many of the leaders in conservation in the last half century, some with little renown but great achievement. They went about their work with uncommon devotion and zeal. They were important personages in their own areas and fields of endeavor. I developed an urge to write about them and about the field of wildlife biology.

I have selected people, projects, and issues in which I participated over the past fifty years and present them in a sequence roughly matching major stages in my life. My purpose is not to tout personal achievements but to relate experiences and describe what it was like to work as a field biologist and nature conservationist. The sections on further reading include some of the material I have published.

If there is a special audience for this book, it is the students in wildlife conservation and management programs in the universities that offer such training. In returning to the classroom in later years, I was struck by the brilliant but often nascent minds of students who delve into the most complicated secrets of science and nature. I also noted a sort of malaise or apathy in some students enrolled as degree candidates in conservation science. Hence I wanted to write about committed conservationists and their projects to give young people insights about the field they are studying.

I also wanted to share what I have learned about the cultural dimensions of societies that are often the root of conservation problems and are essential to solutions. As a young student, I realized that the world is often shaped less by design than by terrible neglect, profligacy, greed—and accidents. As I took on assignments at the global scale, the social, political, and economic conditions of many societies were stinging discoveries. The human condition was always the backdrop to my conservation efforts, and I learned early that people had to be considered in plans for the natural world, or else conservation efforts would likely fail.

Writing about all this in a personal way, I have reexamined the life I knew as a biologist and resurrected memories of conservation affairs long sequestered in my mind. That was the gift of writing this sort of memoir.

One final word: the title of this book, *It's a Long Way from Llano*, commemorates the happiness we discovered when residing in Llano, Texas, and the Central Mineral Region. It may suggest to some that we were happy to leave the town and region after residing there for six years. Far from it, we could not have found more natural beauty, interesting environments and people than in Llano. It was the Valhalla and Nirvana of our lives. There, Joan and I began our marriage, welcomed our first-born, began our careers, and discovered the interface between conservation and people. It was more a home than any we had. We miss it even now after fifty years have passed.

When those of us who worked together as biologists in Llano meet now as old men, one of us usually exclaims, "It's a long way from Llano." It reflects our feelings for the region and recognizes how far we have traveled since leaving it. Llano was the genesis and engine of our careers.

ACKNOWLEDGMENTS

WRITING IN the first person singular may give the impression that I had little assistance or support. Nothing could be further from the truth. I owe much to associates, students, and family. I was always a member of a team of biologists and conservationists. I thank those with whom I worked and hope I have gotten things right.

My wife, Joan Marie Powell Teer, and I were wed more than fifty years ago on March 26, 1955. Joan was born and reared in Mississippi and had all the social graces and manners of the old South. We married during my first year at Madison, Wisconsin, after she completed her B.S. degree at Mississippi Southern University. We welcomed our first child almost exactly on the first anniversary of our wedding. Nothing encouraged me more nor was more important than having a loving wife dedicated to her husband and marriage and to securing our future as a team. As a farm boy with little interest or skill in climbing social ladders or attaining high position, I needed her more than ever. She re-tailored me to her standards, for which I am forever grateful. A few rough spots remain, and she continues to work on them.

So I consider my wife's contributions to my career as important as my university education. She simply was the driving force in my work. Without her support, I could not have successfully completed the many years of training. She and my children have been with me every step of the way. Joan's reasoning and judgments have clearly been more valuable than mine. She is the reason I have written this book. It is dedicated to her and our two children, James W. Teer and Jill M. Teer Epstein, and to my late mother, Mary Ella Teer. They followed, supported, and steered me in whatever directions my career took; they were the principal reasons for success. Without them, I was and am nothing.

My students and colleagues were valuable in many ways, not the least being their friendship. I have aimed to recognize several of them in these essays. They were family as well.

Shannon Davies, Louise Lindsey Merrick Editor for the Natural Environment at Texas A&M University Press, was helpful in every way an editor can be. She was responsible for my accepting the assignment and was the key in carrying it to completion. Without her, I probably would have hung it up after the first chapter.

Dan Pedrotti, Richard Conolly, and the Rotary Club of Corpus Christi provided funds through its Harvey Weil Sportsman Conservation Program, which provided for the use of color photos in the book. I am grateful to them and to project editor Jennifer Ann Hobson and others at Texas A&M University Press for their work in bringing the book to print.

I trust the errors and exaggerations are not too frequent or egregious. If they are, I invite those who discover them to correct them with my blessing.

IT'S A LONG WAY FROM LLANO

Born in the 1920s and raised during the depression, I had my life shaped not only by the natural world but also by the GI Bill following my discharge from the U.S. Navy after World War II.

CHAPTER ONE

The Beginning

MY MOTHER, Mary Ella Dohoney Teer, gave birth to me in our home in the Czech community of Granger, Texas, on March 13, 1926. Dr. M. R. Sharp and two women who served as midwives in the community attended my birth. Our home had only coal oil (kerosene) lamps for light—very poor for the task, especially since I was born at 4:15 A.M. My father, Thomas Lee Teer, placed his automobile at the window of the room to focus its lights on the birthing "bed." My birth was the third to occur on the kitchen table in our home. Two of my three older brothers, Winston and Tom, or T. L. as the family called him, had preceded me there.

Nothing unusual in the cosmos announced my coming, and nothing unusual in my passages through various ages and into my teenage years revealed a predestined life. I was just one of many boys and girls born into an agrarian society in the two or three decades before World War II. Any predestination for any of us was overshadowed by the war, which caught most of my high school classmates and me when we reached draft age for military service. Many years later, I learned that most of the males in my class was in military service within three months after graduation. Several never returned. Until then, I was just another boy whose future and aspirations were played out in poverty and a hardscrabble life. I had little knowledge of worldly things outside a rural environment dominated by a parochial agrarian culture.

My mother kept our family together. She cared for our vegetable garden, fed our animals, and worked as a salesperson on Fridays and Saturdays in a variety store in Granger, peddling cosmetics and hosiery to faithful customers. My job was to deliver the goods she sold and collect payment for them. My father left us—destitute and without any means of support—in 1931 when I was five. He died when I was eight. During the depression years the county usually had food and clothing for poor families, but Mama refused to take charity of any kind. Her pride was immeasurable. We warded off the prospect of "the orphans' home" with my mother's vow, made soon after she was widowed, that we would never be sent there. In retrospect, our family—all of us—had hard times; but happiness permeated our lives and prepared us for independence and a bright future.

Row-crop agriculture was the major land use on the farms. All members of the families who owned land or hired out as day laborers were tied to the land. Cotton, corn, and maize, were the principal crops alongside raising livestock. From the earliest ages, we became well acquainted with these crops. Picking cotton, pulling corn, and cutting maize were the worst of stoop labor. Perhaps the very worst was cutting sorghum cane and removing its leaves to prepare it for the syrup mill. Every day we staked our cow, Helen, on a long chain tethered to an iron stake along roadsides where Johnsongrass and other kinds of forage were plentiful.

Weather, insects, Johnsongrass, weeds, and the vagaries of the market for farmers' produce were responsible for good and bad times. Most families lived almost solely on their own produce, buying only staples and essentials from the stores. When they shopped in town, they usually brought with them eggs, cream, chickens, and vegetables to trade for their staples. Many returned home with a few more cents than they had taken to town. Wives usually had a cookie jar or some such receptacle in which to deposit their change. It was often a source of money to satisfy some small need of the family.

I never learned if the thrifty habits of the people in the region were due to their Czech origins or if thrift was simply forced on them by the economy of the times. One attribute was obvious: clean farms—those with few weeds, little Johnsongrass, and ordered rows and fields—were usually Czech farms. They stood out among all others. Nonetheless, farming was a hard life for all who owned and farmed their own land and especially hard for those who sharecropped it. Most people usually borrowed money to put in their crops in the spring and returned it to the bank in the late fall with little extra when the crops were harvested. Generation after generation of families farmed the same land. Few escaped the tough times until World War II ended and the economy strengthened.

The town and its people were divided by the Missouri, Kansas and Texas Railroad tracks, which split the town almost in half, and by the religions the inhabitants practiced. The Czech people lived on the west side of the tracks, the "Americans" on the east side. Most Czechs were Catholic and the rest were Protestants, usually Baptists, Methodists, and members of the Church of Christ. Differences in religion and culture were magnified by separate schools for Catholics and Protestants. Young boys declared war on one another. Fights, usually little worse than wrestling matches and mud ball fights, often erupted when the public and parochial schools let out for the day and the students were walking home, many to homes more than a few miles distant. Sometimes, however, animosity ran high at some function or sports contest.

I had a habit of "rocking" the horse-drawn milk delivery wagon and the Czech boy who delivered the milk from the wagon to our porch. For a time he dodged my missiles and taunts. Then one day, his boss advised him on how to end this devilment. Cyril Wolf left the wagon, ran straight for me, caught me handily, and gave me the licking I deserved. That ended our war. I had a tough time convincing my companions that my black eye was due to a fall. Cyril and I had a great laugh remembering the event at the fiftieth reunion of our high school graduating class.

My future was shaped by the rural environment in which the natural world was the major source of my interest and pleasure. None in my family had attended college or become acquainted with "careers." People simply had jobs, which were often not continuous or secure. Their knowledge about such things, like mine, was limited by their experiences. Thus I had little advice from them. The G.I. Bill was perhaps the most important source of information about college and the careers that could be followed through study. The bill transformed the latent talent and intellect of many young men and women—without its support we would have been unable to attend college. It was the doorway to my future.

We ultimately became what we knew. Many of us followed hunting and fishing into careers in wildlife biology and conservation because we knew the natural world and liked it. I can still remember the first insect I collected and preserved. It was a large, elongated beetle on the pink flower of a Texas thistle. I knew where my father kept his whiskey, so I took a few drops and preserved my beetle in a half-pint mason jar. For many months I kept it and wondered what more I could learn from collecting and identifying other life forms around me. Purpose entered my life with that beetle. I began to search for and study all kinds of life, large and small, benign and hostile, pretty and not so pretty.

Creeks and rivers meandering through the prairie blacklands near Granger were the playgrounds of youth. They were fringed by woodlands on either side, some more than half a mile in width and grazed by domestic livestock. The creeks had fish, primarily channel and flathead catfish, sun perch, gaspergou, and bass. The woodlands were the major habitats of small game. Riparian vegetation alongside the streams was the favored habitat of squirrels and rabbits. Cultivated land was poor wildlife habitat. Livestock and the plow rendered it almost devoid of food for wildlife and thus virtually a desert for them.

I trapped furbearers—raccoons, opossums, skunks, mink, and sometimes wild house cats—and sold their pelts for pin money. Most of what I received was used to buy .22-caliber short cartridges, which at the time sold at three for one cent. I can still identify the smell of a box of Remington Kleenbore, Kleenkote .22 shells. It has carried with me all these years.

Except for the season when native pecans matured, usually from late September through November, we were welcome to hunt and fish on private land. We gathered pecans "on the halves" and sold our half at local feed stores. Without such arrangements, we were not welcome on the land with creeks and rivers. If you have raided peach orchards, watermelon fields, or pecan groves, you know that money was not the reason for our forays. The fun was to evade closely watched orchards and fields and to come away with the fruit of the farmers' labors.

No melon, peach, or plum from the grocery tasted as good as fruit taken on a moonlight night from a field we knew was being watched by the owner. When occasionally caught, we were in for lectures that seemed never to end. The ladies of the town were on record expecting all the little heathens to end up in prison by the time we were fifteen. But it was a game played by farmers and youth alike. The harm done to our farmer friends was negligible and was soon forgotten, especially if one of us starred on the Granger High School football team.

I cannot say our young lives were idyllic or carefree, but we were about as happy as boys could be. Those days shaped my future and gave me the route to a lifetime of pleasure and, I believe, a redeeming social value in my career.

GRANGER, TEXAS

Granger was one of many small towns dotting the blackland prairie landscape of Central Texas. Farming was the major industry, and activity varied with the planting and harvest seasons. The towns were spaced about fifteen miles apart to serve the agricultural community with cotton gins and the usual feed and seed stores. They were generally sleepy villages through most of the year. After the land was "laid out"—plowed and prepared for spring planting—farmers spent the winter months in more leisurely ways. They repaired equipment, worked with their animals, and did the things that the family wanted in their homes and surroundings.

Many played dominoes and tarot, a card game from Eastern Europe, in the saloons and beer joints that lined main streets of most villages. Granger was a heavily Catholic Czech community, and the amount of beer served there was prodigious. Dances and parties were enjoyed by young and old alike. While the teenagers danced, their fathers were usually in the saloons on the ground floor playing games and drinking beer. Their mothers sat in chairs against the walls of the dance floor to watch and to make sure everything was done properly.

Summer brought watermelon season and the annual sport of stealing fruit; Czech girls, reputed to be the prettiest in the world, were at the top of our interest throughout the year.

At harvest time in the early fall, farming activity intensified. Literally hundreds of itinerant or migrant workers converged on Granger and other small villages to harvest the crops. On Saturdays or when weather forced workers out of the fields, they came to town to replenish their supplies and make contacts and arrangements for work as the season progressed and the cotton matured. On those days Granger was alive with people. Practically every parking space on Main Street and in local parks set aside for them was occupied by families of migrant workers. Stores were exceptionally busy; more than half of their income was received during the harvest season.

Alcohol and fights were usually a part of the Saturday visits to town. A few of the migrant workers drank themselves into a stupor and were incarcerated in a filthy one-room cinder-block jail to sleep it off. On Sunday morning most were returned to the farms where they worked. Some did not sleep but yelled most of the night for someone to release them or bring more beer. We teenagers found them a curious bunch, and I think we learned to avoid the kind of hilarity that seemed to end so badly.

The harvest took the migrants the length of Texas as cotton matured in the late summer and fall. Starting in the Rio Grande Valley, they continued up through the blacklands of South and Central Texas and ultimately ended their journey in the irrigated cropland of the High Plains. Some continued into Oklahoma, Arkansas, and New Mexico. Many of the migrant worker families were in travel and work from September through February. Unlike the ethnic composition of migrant workers today, most were white families who traveled as a unit. Children worked alongside their parents. Now, migrants are much fewer in number and mostly Hispanic. Harvesting and farming in general were done with stoop labor.

Mechanization of harvest machinery was responsible for the reduction in migrant labor in Texas and neighboring states. Mechanical cotton pickers, combines for corn, and other machinery were not yet known when I was growing up. World War II passed before cotton was harvested largely with mechanical pickers. I read John Steinbeck's *Grapes of Wrath* as a teenager and could relate to the Okies and Texans attempting to make their lives worthwhile in the worst of conditions. Their lives were practically the same as those of migrant workers in my time in Central Texas. I now believe the lean lives of those migrant workers and the hard work and uncertainties of the farmers were reasons I did not choose agriculture as a career.

A BOY'S WORLD

I was wedded to nature through enjoyment and use of resources that came from the land, even if I did not fully understand the reasons for my interest at the time. Much of it was due to the freedom and independence that youth seeks in growing into adulthood. Rivers, creeks, bottomlands, and woodlots had few boundaries or limitations. They were available to rural boys, and there was little else to occupy our time. Our parents worried about us, but it was for reasons other than the kinds of things that tempt youth today. If we were not always models of decorum and good conduct, at least there was no guile or meanness in our transgressions.

We spent much of our free time on the San Gabriel River. It snaked and meandered through the blackland prairies and had large trees along its course. I considered it my river. It was about four miles from our house. Aside from our bicycles used in our paper routes, we had no transportation. We walked the four miles to the river in about two hours, lugging our camp gear and bedding. Just thinking about walking into a stiff January norther on our return home makes my head ache and brings tears of stinging cold to my eyes.

With the most primitive materials, we built several boats over the years. These were usually made from sheets of corrugated iron (tin) tacked on to wooden sides and caulked with tar wherever seams required it. Because tin sheets usually come in ten- to twelve-foot lengths, our boats were ten to twelve feet long. At most they could carry two people, and water was usually two or three inches from the gunwale. Paddles were homemade from scrap lumber; their weight and design left us weary and frustrated by their use. The boats floated, but that is about all that can be said for them. A serious problem occurred when we had to carry these makeshift craft from Granger to Willis Creek, almost a mile from our home. We usually abandoned the boats after a time or they washed away from heavy rains that put the river out of its banks. We would make new ones after such losses, but we never achieved what we desired in our craft.

We spent happy hours and made many discoveries at Willis Creek and the San Gabriel River. We swam, fished, hunted, built fires to warm ourselves, roasted meadowlarks and robins over our fires, and on occasion stole a few pecans from the farmers' woodlands.

In warmer weather, anything above sixty-five degrees, we usually ended up at the "blue hole," our favorite swimming hole on Willis Creek. Often we camped there, spreading our quilts at its very edge. In season, our walk to the creek was interrupted by choosing a watermelon or two from Mr. Puckett's patch. We carried them with us, put them in the water to cool for several hours, and ate them like hungry wolves in the late afternoon.

A swing tied to a long rope and attached to a tree overhanging the deep, blue water was the center of our play. We took turns launching ourselves from the bank, swinging out over the water and dropping, feet or head first, into the deep pool. Naked as a picked bird and with a great Tarzan yell, we would drop into the blue hole as far out from the bank as we could. Swimming at the blue hole was all elation and unabashed joy. Well, almost all. Anyone who has seen the television sitcom *Seinfeld* understands George Constanza's embarrassment over shrinkage. A few boys, usually the larger ones, were "bank walkers." The smaller boys stayed in the water, measuring its depth from time to time with the words, "peter deep, peter deep," always good for a laugh.

From age twelve, I hunted with a .22 rifle. My brothers taught me to hunt. I was permitted to hunt with them as long as I "minded" them and carried our game. In the blackland prairies and river bottoms of Central Texas our game was mainly rabbits and squirrels. My friends and I trapped raccoons, opossums, minks, and even skunks for their fur. I was once asked to leave school after a successful night of taking a family of skunks in our barn. Skinned and with hides stretched, skunks brought about 50 cents; raccoons, $5; opossums, $1; and mink, rarely caught, $10.

I soon learned that a feral house cat, of which there were many, was likely to bite and scratch you when attempts were made to release one caught in a steel trap. Cats were dumped by city folks in wild places. They were efficient predators and, like boys, a serious menace to small birds and mammals. I caught a large, coal-black cat with yellow eyes. It was mad and hurting. Gingerly, and with the help of a large limb placed over its neck to pin the cat to the ground, I was successful in releasing it from the steel jaws of the trap, but not without receiving severe scratches, lacerations, and bites on both my arms. Teeth and claws seemed to be everywhere. Most trappers simply shot them.

The first rifle I owned was a used .22 rimfire Stevens single shot purchased from Baca and Bohac's hardware in Granger for $2.50. It could take short and long cartridges in its short chamber, but not long-rifle cartridges. It had a rolling block receiver to load the cartridges and eject the spent hulls. I paid for the rifle at 25 cents per week. Pride of ownership of the finest firearm available today could not match the pride I had in that little .22. Unfortunately, it was lost during the time I was in the navy.

We always seemed to be out of ammunition. One of my best boyhood friends, August Prcin, and I once went to the hardware store together to buy bullets for our .22s. For several minutes no one came to wait on us. So we decided to help ourselves by reaching over the counter and stuffing our pockets with boxes of .22 cartridges—until we realized that the owner was watching us from behind a refrigerator. We returned the shells as quickly as we could, fearing all the while that he would have us put in jail or at least give us a good whipping and lecture. Fortunately, he did neither. In my adult life, Mr. Baca and I laughed about the incident on many occasions. He understood the desperate needs of young boys sojourning in nature with a gun but without shells.

We learned the loops and deep holes of the river and the sections of streamside vegetation that offered the best hunting and fishing. We knew which hollow trees could be depended upon to harbor a raccoon or opossum almost every time we went there. Visits to those trees were made as faithfully as a trapper visits his sets. We learned sign—tracks, dens, prey, loafing, and escape cover and how to use it for tracking and hunting. One of my favorite den trees was a big sycamore with a den in the fork of its largest limbs. The sycamore and one other large tree I admired, a pecan, remain as they did when I was a boy. I visit them now and then to relive our relationship.

At night we hunted with carbide lights (miners' lamps) to locate the eyes of animals in trees and brush along the streams. We spent about as much time cleaning the clogged orifices of carbide lights from which the flame came as the amount of time they functioned properly. A small length of wire from a window screen was absolutely necessary to clean the porcelain orifice.

The dim light gave an eerie feeling as we walked through the woodlands looking for the eyes of "varmints." On one dark winter night, the weirdest scream I have heard in my life shook and scared August and me into full flight. To this day, I cannot identify it, and none whom I've asked can either. It was an animal—a bird or a mammal but not a human, although at the time we speculated that someone was attempting to terrify us. Whatever or whoever screamed, it scared us out of our wits. As soon as we could recover, we raced back to our camp where we built a roaring fire. Carbide lights were not very efficient but operated at low cost; they were considerably cheaper than battery-powered lights. A large floodlight would have been welcome that eerie night!

We fished for catfish with rod and reel but mostly with drop lines, throw lines, and occasionally trot lines. Sets were baited with "red horse minners," sunfish or perch, chicken livers, and sometimes earthworms. Lines were checked with a "run" at about three-hour intervals during the night. We slept on a pallet in quilts made by our mothers. Only rich kids and adults had sleeping bags.

I knew nothing about spin casting and certainly nothing about fly fishing. Modern tackle had not arrived in our town, and when it did, it did not capture me or it was too expensive to own. City kids who were a little too proud of their tackle and who poked fun at our old rods and reels were asked, "Do you want to fish like a gentleman or do you want to catch some fish?" It was a put-down that worked every time.

Nature was more enjoyable than other organized activities available at the time, though most boys played football. Friday-night football was a show, a major interest to the townspeople. The town barber, old Dewey Ball, gave a free haircut to any player who made a spectacular play. Football permitted us to posture to attract girls. I suspect, however, that every one of us led virginal lives until graduating from high school. Yet sports, picture shows, books, carnivals, circuses, and church did not compete with our escapes to the rivers and creeks.

I did not burden my thoughts with the weighty matters that influence conservation of living resources today. I did not know about overwhelming human numbers, over-exploitation of large mammals and game birds, ecological paradigms, or habitat abuse afflicting this or that species; I did not wonder whether recreational hunting was justified or merely blood sport. We were callous at times. Conservation of wildlife could have been much more efficient if .22 rifles had been regulated for certain uses. Once I shot a great blue heron at its nest in a large rookery on the San Gabriel just to see it up close. On another occasion, I shot a beaver that had been dislodged from its home on the bank of the Colorado River by flood water, again only to see it up close. Boys did those things and regretted them afterward.

As a youth, I had not been made aware of the order and purity of the natural world. As far as I knew, it was just there for our use and enjoyment. I did not know the first thing about megafauna; it was not in my vocabulary. Nor did I know anything of the African and Indian large mammals that would entice me to foreign lands and keep me away from home for frequent and extended periods. I did not think about trophy deer with antlers measuring twenty-four inches on the inside spread or giant tuskers with ninety-pound ivory on each side. None of these occurred on Willis Creek or the San Gabriel River. We were satisfied with what was in our world and did not worry about other regions or animals.

Nothing about my life was as absolute or as clear as the natural world was in my youth. I am thankful that the fascination and glory of it never left me.

MY RIVER

So you could say that I had a river, the San Gabriel, in Williamson County, to which I owe much of my happiness and certainly my career. It was a beautiful stream that flowed blue-green over calcium carbonate and serpentine rocks of the Edwards Plateau and blackland prairies. It slowed over splendid shoals and gravel bars and paused in deep, dark pools. It made its journey under an almost complete canopy of trees that offered cool shelter to those who visited, a lush contrast to the cultivated heavy prairie soils through which it made its way to the sea. Life was plentiful and interesting there.

After I left home permanently at age eighteen to join the navy, I often thought about the San Gabriel. I always planned to revisit it when I returned after the war. When I could, I did, but those times were few and brief. Nonetheless, the river was always there, and the fact it was there offered recompense and pleasure.

During a long sojourn in the Marianas Islands during World War II, I regularly visited my boyhood friend August Prcin, who was stationed as a young sailor on a floating dry dock (ABSD 2) moored in the harbor at Guam. I was also stationed in Guam. Our visits were often spent planning a canoe trip. We planned to start at Mankins Crossing, a low water crossing on the San Gabriel near Georgetown, and to continue down Little River and the Brazos River to the Gulf of Mexico. Thinking about the trip was a welcome respite from long, lonely days an ocean away from home. My river was a comfort and leveling influence. We never made the trip after the war. Life's demands caught up with us, canoe trips were lost among our efforts to establish ourselves and our families, and August died at a young age. But memories of the San Gabriel never left me.

Biologists, especially old, experienced biologists, are prone to reliving their experiences with philosophical wanderings and lamentations about things past. We seem to have an oversupply of dire consequences if society does not change its ways; we complain about the degradation and loss of wildlife of special interest to people, and younger biologists with budding careers may view all this as defensive posturing. I fear I am one of those old biologists, and I ask your indulgence. I am, after all, long in the tooth and have witnessed changes that indeed put wildlife at risk of complete loss.

We all have places of exceptional beauty or significance in our lives, places held dear in our hearts and usually connected to nature and where we grew up. People living in New York or New Jersey may have deep feelings about Yankee Stadium or Flushing Meadows or natural areas such as Old Cape May and the many refuges on the eastern seaboard. Such treasures are held in memory through a lifetime, though they may be seldom visited. To know they are there is enough. They give pleasure and a sense of geography to our lives.

In *Lonesome Dove*, Larry McMurtry describes Augustus McCrae's love for Claire. Life's demands make visits with her infrequent and brief. Mortally wounded by Indians on a trail drive to Montana, Gus asks his friend, Captain Call, to return his body to a particular spot by a beautiful tree-lined stream where he and Claire once spent a few hours. Captain Call carries his friend's remains on a two-wheeled cart from Montana to the special place in Texas that meant so much to Augustus even though for most of his life, Gus could see that place and Claire only in his memories.

Beauty and significance are held as lifelong treasures. We never release them. The San Gabriel River in Williamson County was my special place. Yet memory sometimes serves us better than reality. Today, like many other Texas rivers and their tributaries, my river can no longer be acclaimed for its pristine and untrammeled beauty. Parts of it have been virtually destroyed by human intemperance with the land through which it courses.

Most of the prairies in my part of Texas had already been converted to cropland by the end of World War II. The riverside vegetation that fringed the San Gabriel and other streams was removed to increase arable land

and cattle pastures. Soil erosion became a major problem despite efforts of government agencies to control it. Fish and wildlife habitat decreased year by year until little woody vegetation remained. The decline in wildlife and fish became evident in our hunting and fishing bags. Now, amid the burgeoning human population along the Interstate 35 corridor in Williamson County, the San Gabriel River enters the city of Georgetown in two streams originating in the Edwards Plateau. They join in the city and continue through the blackland prairie where the San Gabriel meets with Little River. Besides the problem of urban run-off, the city uses the river, as many do, to transport its treated wastewater away from the town. Some undesirable effluents are accidentally or otherwise released into the river.

After several years of not seeing the San Gabriel, in 2002 I took my grandson Lucas on a canoe trip from Mankins Crossing to Circleville, the same stretches of the river I had paddled in my youth. What greeted us was almost unbelievable. The water was turbid. Fish I had seen in the past—catfish of several species, bass, and sunfish—were gone. We saw mostly "trash fish"—carp, suckers, and buffalo. Rocks and bottom were covered with moss, smells were easily identified as waste, and all manner of materials floated on the surface.

The flow of the San Gabriel, even in the spring when it should have been in full spate, was so low that portages over shoals and bars were an almost constant need. The many springs formerly gushing from the river banks were gone or only trickles. Although I did not measure the temperature of the water, the lack of shade from the missing canopy surely made the river several degrees warmer than it used to be. In short, my river was gone. It could not become Lucas's river.

Caring for the earth has to be more than a clever one-liner or entreaty. Somewhere, sometime, somehow, we must live to conserve, or conserve to live.

Wallace Stegner wrote an eloquent essay in 1962 in the *Washington Post* about conservation:

> Something will have gone out of [each of] us as a person if we ever let the remaining wilderness be destroyed; if we permit the last virgin forest to be turned into comic books and plastic cigarette cases; if we drive the few remaining members of the wild species into zoos or to extinction; if we pollute the last clear air and dirty the last clean streams; and push our paved roads through the last of the silence, so that never again will Americans be free in their own country from the noise, the exhausts, the stinks of human and automotive waste, and so that never again can we have the chance to

see ourselves single, separate, vertical, and individual in the world, part of the environment of trees and rocks and soil, brother to the other animals, part of the natural world and competent to belong in it. We simply need that wild country available to us, even if we never do more than drive to its edge and look in. For it can be a means of reassuring ourselves of our sanity as creatures, as part of the geography of hope.

THE HOXIE HOUSE

In the cool of late afternoons and early evenings after working in the fields, doing chores around the house and garden, and tending our livestock, my mother often sat with me and my three brothers on the front porch of our wood-frame house to rest from the day's work and talk about what to do to prepare for school.

Life without a breadwinner—that is, making ends meet for Mama and four boys ranging in age from five to fifteen—was the focus of our lives. All of us worked and helped her keep our family intact. At the end of the harvest season in preparation for the upcoming school year, we measured our success by counting and admiring the clothes we bought from the fruit of our labor. There were stacks of overalls, jeans, shirts, shoes, underclothes, and the like. I can still see the pride and satisfaction on my siblings' and Mama's faces when viewing the result of the summer's work. Our mother worked hardest, yet she seldom bought clothes for herself. With a vegetable garden, a milk cow, chickens, and a pig or two, we lived through the worst of times and kept our pride at being self-sufficient.

Mama often pointed to the southeast and asked, "Do you see it? Do you see the Hoxie House? There it is above the trees a long way away." The Hoxie House was a three-story framed ranch house near the San Gabriel River about ten miles from us. To find the Hoxie House became a game with us.

"Yes, I see it. There it is. I see it." I'm not sure now if any of us could say with certainty that he saw it. I am sure that I did not always see it, although I sometimes said I did. Only the upper third story was visible, but heat shimmer and haze frequently distorted and hid the view. Although I saw the house up close when I hunted and fished along the San Gabriel River, it nevertheless held a sort of mystery when we searched for it from the porch.

Seeing the Hoxie House in our game was not as important as the metaphor it represented in our lives. We didn't understand what Mama was doing. She did. She used it to challenge us to be more than we were. "If you have a clear day, you will see it almost any time," she said. "If you study hard, are honest, fair and responsible, put goals in your lives, and work for what you want, you will see the Hoxie House just about anytime you wish, even on a dark, cloudy day."

As of this writing, two of the four brothers remain—Donald Maurice and me. Mama died in 1985 at age 92, Winston at 79 in 1985, and Tom at 85 in 2005. The men were successful in their work and lives. Mama lived for us and asked nothing for herself. We made certain she was comfortable in her declining years.

The Hoxie House burned to the ground a few years ago. I swear I can see it now or anytime I want to see it. It served a high purpose for Mama and us.

CHAPTER TWO

Into a Man's World

IF THERE was a single crucial time or event that contributed to my maturity, it had to be World War II. As noted, my generation, the "Greatest Generation," according to Tom Brokaw, was drafted into or volunteered for military duty as soon as we graduated from high school. Most of us in rural America had never been outside our states of residence. Many had not been farther than a few miles from home. It was a somber time, but young people found excitement and adventure at every turn. It changed us to adults quite quickly. Many of us entered college on our return to civilian life at the end of the war. Some young men and women had by then developed firm goals, and for those with an interest in nature, wildlife biology was an option, a new field of applied science and management.

WORLD WAR II

When I turned eighteen in March 1944 and joined the U.S. Navy, my tour of duty took me to the Pacific Islands, including Hawaii, Johnson, Guam, and Japan. The war never caught up with me nor I with it, although I spent almost fifteen months in the Pacific Theater. I exerted considerable effort in attempting to work my way to China, but the war ended before I reached that goal. I was stationed on Guam for almost a year and was sent home in January 1946, when the war ended.

There was much time for reflection and planning for the future. The great movie *Mr. Roberts*, starring Henry Fonda, told the story of the boredom and ennui of servicemen and women with duties on islands and ships that serviced the fighting forces. Very soon after landing on Guam in August 1944, I learned what it was like to be away from home with little to occupy the endless days of island life. I was stationed at the Naval Operating Base on Orote Peninsula. Guam was a beautiful island of palm-fringed lagoons with azure skies and water. We could fish and swim in these lagoons but were cautioned about going to the north end of the island, where enterprising Japanese hid in the mountains for years before finally surrendering; one or two remained hidden there for some twenty-five years after the end of World War II.

Years later I made plans to revisit some of the islands where I had served. Guam was first on the list. My dean at the time, Dr. R. C. Potts, had assigned me to go to Japan to review their culture of oysters, shrimp, and other sea creatures. I routed my trip home through Guam. On arrival I was surprised to see tourist developments and resorts on the water's edge, occupied primarily by honeymooners from Japan. Tumon Bay, a favorite, was lined with hotels, condos, and the accoutrements that draw tourists. The Japanese had retaken Guam!

When asked by my grandsons what I did in the "big war," I tell them I was a key man in the First Remingtons or the Second Royals. They have the grace to be overcome with laughter when I explain that I was a typist—the Remingtons and Royals were typewriters, and my war work was on typewriter keys. For a short time, I served as a yeoman for the commander of our unit, the Fleet Records Office on Guam, typing my way through the war as part of a unit that kept records of the duty stations of all sailors in the Pacific Theater so that mail could be delivered to them and they could be located for changes in assignments. It was neither a glorious duty nor an exemplary contribution to the war effort. I merely served where I was assigned, and despite all efforts to be transferred to a more active unit in the war zone, I remained on Guam until the Japanese surrendered. World War II defined my generation, and I was—and am— proud to have been a part of it.

UNIVERSITY TRAINING IN WILDLIFE BIOLOGY

Upon my discharge for the navy, I enrolled at what was then called Texas A&I University in Kingsville and spent four semesters taking core courses in history, mathematics, chemistry, government, and agriculture. The G.I. Bill was a godsend, and I also worked at whatever jobs came my way. I had part-time jobs as a trucker hauling bales of cotton from the gin to the cotton yard, a sort of waiter at the swimming pool snack bar at Texas A&I, a shelf stocker at several grocery stores in Granger and Kingsville, and a clerk at Salm's Tailor and Cleaners.

In the spring of 1947, I met Marvin Lubojasky from Bellville, who was enrolled at Texas A&I. Marvin was usually accompanied by a large dog, a Malamute sled dog he had obtained in Alaska. Alaska was in a boom period and employment in various building trades and services attracted students and tradesmen, especially from the West Coast. Marvin was a quiet, resourceful, young man of Czech descent with a penchant for health foods and body building. He seldom engaged in any hilarity and fun, usually keeping to himself. We admired him, though we did not exchange our sedentary habits for his interest in keeping fit.

ALASKAN ADVENTURES

Marvin and I became friends. We talked a lot about Alaska and employment opportunities there. Alaska spelled money and adventure to me, and I asked if I could go with him when he returned there in the summer of 1947. He agreed. We began planning the trip and equipping ourselves for travel from Kingsville to Anchorage, much of the way on the recently completed, as yet unpaved, Alaska-Canadian Highway, known as the Alcan Highway. I was twenty-one.

The Alcan Highway was built and maintained by the American and Canadian military forces and agencies of the two governments. Its purpose was to enable armed forces to put troops in the Aleutian Islands, which had been invaded by the Japanese in 1943. The highway was ultimately paved along its entire length, and now thousands of tourists and commercial vehicles drive it.

Marvin had a "war-surplus" 1942 Plymouth sedan and a ski trailer (a two-wheel trailer fitted with wheels and skis for use in the far North) he had purchased on his last trip to Alaska. It was perfect for our group, which now consisted of five young men—Marvin and his brother Charlie, my brother Donald and I, and Joe Dalton from San Antonio—and Marvin's Malamute. It was a crowded car and trailer that carried us, our tents, bedding, food, and auto supplies. Seventy gallons of gasoline in five-gallon petrol cans was the minimum amount of fuel required for travel between gas stations.

To travel the Alcan, Canadian authorities required that spares of essential motor parts be carried with us because vast stretches of it had no services. We bought extra water and air pumps, several spare tires and carburetors, first aid kits, and other gear. Except for the tires, none of the spare parts were needed. Flats were frequent on the graveled road, and we were often stuck or slowed by mud. On several occasions we saw eighteen-wheel trucks mired in muddy stretches of the road. No autos and few trucks could pass until the road dried, sometimes requiring three or four days.

We left Kingsville as soon as the semester ended in mid-May and arrived in Anchorage after thirteen days of constant driving. Our route took us through mid-continent to International Falls, Minnesota, where we crossed into Canada, and thence to Calgary and Edmonton, Alberta. At Tok Junction, we left the Alcan Highway and entered Alaska.

It was as great an adventure as we thought it would be. Several events were dangerous and even life threatening, but the beauty of the entire region and the enjoyment of the experiences were more than sufficient payback. Only one constant annoyance ate at our very sanity: mosquitoes. Their numbers were far greater than those of the southern United States. We could eat only while standing in the smoke of a fire, and then only for a few minutes. Swarms of mosquitoes were everywhere. Escape was impossible. Yet the views of mountains and plains, of rushing rivers and deep blue lakes, of bears and beavers, of ducks and swans, and of the northern lights made this problem bearable.

When we came to the Peace River in British Columbia, it was at flood stage as a result of the spring thaw. We had to cross it to continue our journey. A small water-driven ferry operated by a local Scotsman was the only option we had to cross the river. The ferry was not powered by any mechanical device, motor, or draft animal. Such ferries are often seen in remote and under-developed regions of the world. These ferries are powered by the force of the water. By using the rudder to turn the ferry into a position to catch the current, it could be sent across the river on a cable stretched from one bank to the other. The ferry on the Peace River served the region for many years until the mid-1960s, when a bridge was built over the river near Great Slave Lake.

With some trepidation, we loaded ourselves, the car, trailer, and other loose goods onto the ferry. As we cast off, the ferryman turned the rudder to the appropriate angle with the current. The ferry immediately set off toward the opposite bank. Then as we proceeded into the main current, the Malamute walked onto the apron. Joe Dalton immediately followed to get the dog. Their weight pushed the apron down into the water. The water caught the apron, and the force of it began to turn the ferry onto its side. We tried but could not right the ferry. Large timbers to which the apron was attached and hinged broke with a loud crash. Joe and the dog were thrown into the swift, icy water, and the car and trailer began to slide off the ferry. The ferryman finally managed to turn the rudder, right the ferry, and get back to the bank.

Edward L. Kozicky, Walter A. Isbell, and Robert A. McCabe
(above, left to right) and George V. Burger (below) at camp.
Our deep friendships spanned several decades.

Robert J. Kleberg Jr., President of King Ranch, and Rogers C. B. Morton, U.S. Secretary of the Interior. Their support of conservation made much of my work possible.

Close-up of white-winged dove.

Students building and repairing dove traps.

The Camargue horses in southern France.

Nilgai, like this one shown with biologist William Sheffield, are native to India. They do well in South Texas except that they succumb to occasional hard freezes.

Elephants can be lured into areas with water and food. However, as some parks and reserves in Africa have documented, elephants can be crowded into small areas to their disadvantage. More than 3,500 elephants starved in Tsavo National Park in Kenya in the 1960s when there were more elephants than the forage and water could support. The situation was exacerbated when boreholes were provided by well-meaning conservationists and concerned citizens. The addition of water simply attracted more elephants; they stripped the habitat and starved to death.

Reduction cropping of elephants to reduce habitat damage leaves only their bones after they have been processed for valuable parts—tusks, skins, and meat. The bison hunters of the western United States gathered similar mounds of bones during the years when bison were hunted almost to extinction, although in that case no higher impulse to conserve habitat was operating.

Tusks are extremely valuable, and elephants are heavily poached for their ivory. Tusks taken from elephants in reduction cropping operations are removed. Legally taken tusks are either stored or sold, depending on the laws at the time. Tchuma Tchato, a community conservation project in Tete Province of Mozambique, was harassed by elephants. The village was located in an area much used by elephants, and several villagers were wounded or killed each year. The elephants were shot and the ivory was stockpiled with the plan to sell it whenever given permission by the government and the Convention on Threatened and Endangered Species (CITES). The ivory remains in storage.

Lions and herds of large mammals in Africa provide a wildlife spectacle unmatched in variety and beauty. Hunting and tourism are sources of foreign exchange in many nations, producing a large amount of conservation funding. Lions are easily seen in parks and reserves, and they attract visitors.

Controversy surrounds hunting lions and other cats. The chief issue centers on the conflict between the number of lions in protected reserves and the protection of farmers' livestock from predation. Many people simply do not wish to permit lion hunting because of the beauty of the cats.

Herds of saiga occur in the desolate steppes of northern Eurasia and are adapted to cope with the arid conditions and bitter winter cold.

Valeri Neronov, deputy director of the Man and the Biosphere program in Russia, is shown here standing in the desertized blacklands of Kalmykia. Valeri was my primary contact in studies of the saiga antelope in Kalmykia. Logistics, travel arrangements, and fluent Russian were absolutely necessary to the project. Without his friendship and interest in the saiga, we could not have worked in Russia.

Field party of Russian (Kalmykia) and American biologists at lunch.

We were sure we had lost Joe and the Malamute. The current carried both down the river for about two miles. Joe wore cowboy boots and a large leather jacket that we surmised would surely drown him. A great dread came over us. The ferryman yelled to his family across the river for help. Immediately several people raced to the river to find Joe. They found him washed up on a flooded gravel bar, unable to get out of the shallow water. The men carried him to their home to thaw out. The dog was rescued with him.

A tragedy was averted. When we next saw Joe, he was sitting in an easy chair in the ferryman's house, drinking a glass of Scotch whiskey and smiling. We scolded him about stepping onto the apron to get the dog, but any one of us would have done what Joe did. The ferryman repaired the ferry, and we proceeded to our destination two days later.

A few days after this episode, the tents and other goods in the ski trailer caught fire. One of us had flipped a cigarette out of the car window, and it landed in the trailer. We saw smoke, and then a blaze erupted. Every one of us was galvanized to get the gasoline out of the trailer. We pulled the tins out and flung them as far away as possible. The tents were treated with paraffin and were especially flammable. We got the gasoline out, but at great risk. A good assortment of our gear and supplies was destroyed.

On our arrival in Anchorage, each of us found employment almost immediately. For about a month I worked as a "gandy dancer" on the Alaska Railroad. (A gandy dancer lays and repairs track, builds and repairs bridges, and clears debris from the tracks and rights-of-away). It was tough work. Most who took jobs with the state-owned railroad were Indians who lived rough and dissipated lives. I learned that "green tobacco" was marijuana and that most workers used it and other substances on the job as well as during down times. Indians were drunk in the evenings. We lived with them in the "Snake Pit," a Quonset hut provided by the railroad. I was befriended by one of the Indians, who looked after me when fighting erupted. Even so, danger in that hut was palpable. I soon searched for better living conditions as well as better pay.

After a month of employment with the Alaskan Railroad, my brother and I joined the International Longshoreman's Union (ILA), a requirement to work on the docks. The pay was much better, and it was safer than the Snake Pit. We were soon accepted by the dock workers and learned to handle cargo—lumber, drums of gasoline and oil, foodstuffs, and many other items not made or grown in Alaska. Unloading ships and barges in Cook Inlet was hard work too, and the weather was often cold and rainy. We wore rain gear and warm clothes, which never seemed to be quite enough. There was no respite in our work day; we worked ten hours every day of the week.

Consequently, we saw very little of Alaska. Our wanderings were confined to about fifty miles around Anchorage. When we had a few hours for ourselves, we visited the harbor where fishing vessels were moored and the sheds where fish and crustaceans were processed. We sometimes fished for salmon in Ship Creek, which coursed through Anchorage proper. Coho and other species of salmon were abundant during their migration and spawning seasons. We soon learned to catch them on treble hooks attached to long lines that were thrown in and jerked through the water to impale them, a technique legal at the time but now illegal. So numerous were the salmon that we rarely failed to catch one on each cast. We grilled or fried our catch on a gravel bar of Ship Creek, a pleasant late afternoon escape from the heavy work on the docks.

The tide in Cook Inlet has a range of twenty-six feet, exceeded in North America only by the tides in the Bay of Fundy in Newfoundland, which holds the record. Coming into the narrow inlet with the tide was almost a sure way to lose control of the ship. It was never done by knowledgeable captains.

On one occasion, a Greek ship came into the inlet with the tide. Every longshoreman on the dock attempted to waive the ship off, but it was too late. It plowed into a barge unloading lumber at the dock and cut the barge in two. It continued into the dock for about thirty yards before it hit and rested at the railroad leading onto the docks. Longshoremen on the barge, my brother among them, were thrown into the water but were recovered about a mile downstream with the tide. Miraculously, no one was lost. All were rescued, some with injuries. I was working in one of the railroad cars receiving lumber. I will never forget the ship looming over me as it sliced slowly but inexorably through the dock, throwing large dock timbers here and there as it proceeded.

We had planned to return to Texas A&I for the fall session. However, we were making more money than we had ever made, and our finances for college were increasing. So we stayed on the job until Cook Inlet froze in early December. We flew home!

I did not go back to Alaska to work, as my brother did for the next two years. He was a law student at Baylor University and worked in the summer as a longshoreman in the Aleutian Islands in 1948 and as a "powder monkey" in 1949, blasting rock to make roads in parts of the interior of Alaska. Sometimes I wonder where I could have learned more than in the

Alaska experience. Although I never again saw any of my Alaska friends after I left college, every student should have such experiences. In 1992, I returned to Anchorage to receive the Aldo Leopold Memorial Medal for conservation achievement from the Wildlife Society, an honor of which I am most proud.

TEXAS A&M UNIVERSITY

Because Texas A&I (now Texas A&M University–Kingsville) did not offer a degree in wildlife biology, I transferred to Texas A&M University in College Station in 1948, where I obtained a B.S. degree in 1950. The Department of Wildlife Management at Texas A&M was one of the nation's first, and the school was among the most prominent universities to offer an education in wildlife biology and management. As part of the land grant system, the university and department were staffed by several eminent scientist-educators, including Dr. W. B. Davis, Dr. Leonard Wing, and Dr. Wendell G. Swank. They were the greatest classroom and field studies professors I had in my university years. Because of their reputations and the army of servicemen and women returning after World War II, the Department of Wildlife Management at Texas A&M was almost overwhelmed with students. Studying there anchored my formal education securely.

The G.I. Bill provided funds for my bachelor's degree, just as the bill made it possible for thousands of other World War II veterans to be educated in their chosen field at the university or training program of their choice. It was the most far-reaching and important benefit imaginable. Tuition, books, and subsistence were the major provisions of the bill. Over the years, millions of people have taken advantage of the chance this offered. Without it, I am sure I would not have had the chance to attend college.

In 1950, my class graduated with about thirty students. Enrollments continued to increase through the 1970s, with more than 750 undergraduates and 75 graduate students enrolled in wildlife management following Earth Day in 1970. Unfortunately, students graduating during these peak years outnumbered the jobs available by a wide margin, and some changed their careers out of necessity. However, the number of graduates was important to the cause of conservation because they infused their knowledge about wildlife into society. Many became volunteers for non-government conservation organizations, which were just beginning to be formed and felt in conservation circles. Wildlife biologists trained in this

Wildlife biologists are attracted to the profession by the beauty, order, and truths of the natural world. I began my career in 1948 when I first enrolled at Texas A&M University—as yet unaware that biologists are often faced with bitter and deep-seated differences among the people interested in wildlife.

era were among the pioneers in scientific management. They formed the foundation of the conservation movement.

Iowa State University

After receiving my B.S. degree in the summer of 1952, I began searching for a position in wildlife management with state and national conservation agencies. My academic record was good. Like many graduates of the time, I applied for every position that came to my attention. Failing to find one, I turned to continuing my education with graduate studies.

Iowa State University advertised for a graduate student position to work on waterfowl in the marshes of southwestern Iowa. I immediately called Dr. Halbert Harris, chairman of the Department of Zoology and Entomology, and asked to be considered for the position. He instructed me to apply, and I was chosen for the two-year project.

Dr. Edward L. Kozicky, then leader of the Iowa Cooperative Wildlife Research Unit, was assigned as my major advisor. He came to be a life-long friend and colleague in wildlife affairs. A Coop Unit fellowship was provided to me by the U.S. Fish and Wildlife Service through its cooperative research program at Iowa State. Dr. George O. Hendrickson and Dr. Kenneth D. Carlander were great teachers in their respective fields—Hendrickson in ecology and wildlife management and Carlander in fisheries.

Forney, a small village in Fremont County in southwest Iowa, about thirty-five miles south of Council Bluffs, was my study area. This large oxbow lake of the Missouri River was a favorite hunting marsh for mallards and other pond ducks. However, it was being overhunted and few ducks were taken. Hunters were unable to get clean shots because competition was so great.

The Iowa Conservation Commission decided to regulate the competition in 1951 by reducing the number of hunters allowed on the marsh at any one time and to reduce "sky-shooting" (shooting at ducks out of range) by those who did gain entry. A lottery was used to select hunters. Hunting was permitted every other day, and a fourth day on weekends. Blinds were built for the hunters, and wardens patrolled the marsh to reduce sky-shooting

Management of the marsh and the hunters who used it was a decided improvement, ensuring both a great mallard habitat and good hunting. In addition to management, I was required to sex and age all ducks in the hunters' bags and to record migration of ducks and geese through the area. I was able to determine arrival and departure times of the major species and provide these data to the U.S. Fish and Wildlife Service, which set seasons, bag limits, and means and methods of hunting. I enjoyed the project, as waterfowl and marshes were my favored research topic in those early days.

In March and April each year, thousands of snow geese roosted at Forney Lake for several weeks during their northward return migration to their breeding grounds in James Bay. They left the lake soon after daybreak, fed on waste grain in adjacent fields, and returned to the marsh near dusk. On several occasions I counted more than 250,000 snow and blue geese, color phases of the same species, in residence at the marsh edge. While field feeding, they appeared as a huge white blanket spread over the landscape. It truly was a magnificent wildlife spectacle.

Great flocks of mallards also used the marsh. They, too, were attracted by the waste grain. I remember with pleasure the flocks of mallards circling and wheeling, their wings cutting the air, "talking" as they set their wings to land.

From the beginning of my formal education, I planned to earn my doctorate at the University of Wisconsin. Aldo Leopold was the major attraction for students to study there. The Department of Wildlife Ecology at Wisconsin was usually ranked in the top ten wildlife programs in the country, and only a few graduate students were accepted there each year. Before entering ISU, I had spoken with Bob McCabe, one of Leopold's students and his assistant in research, about my interest in the department. He advised me to get my master's degree at some other university, which I did. After completing it, I applied for admission to the University of Wisconsin and was eventually accepted. However, Leopold had died fighting a grass fire in 1948, and I missed him by five years. McCabe agreed to take me as one of his students, a fortunate decision for me. Failing to obtain a place with Leopold, I thought the next best position would be to study under someone whose career and work had been shaped by him.

The University of Wisconsin provided funds for my graduate studies at Madison, awarding a Wisconsin Alumni Research Foundation scholarship and grant from the Aldo Leopold Green Tree Garden Club of Milwaukee. In addition, the Delta Waterfowl Research Station at Delta, Manitoba, provided money for an internship on a predation project in its marshes.

DELTA WATERFOWL RESEARCH STATION

Waterfowl had always been a part of my life. Throughout my youth and college years, I was interested in waterfowl and wetlands. I was fascinated by the millions of ducks and geese that migrated annually between their nesting grounds in the prairie wetlands of Canada, often referred to as the "duck factories" of North America, and their winter homes in the southern United States and Mexico. Once I kept a small flock of free-ranging pond ducks in my yard simply to observe them, not in rigorous behavioral and ecological studies but as creatures epitomizing how physical form and function fitted them for their interesting lives. I hunted ducks and geese in the coastal marshes and bays of Texas. They remained a lifelong interest, although there were frequent periods in which I had little opportunity to study or hunt them.

The great drought of the 1930s throughout most of the prairie provinces of Canada and the nesting areas of the United States imperiled continental populations of waterfowl. The Dust Bowl or Duck Depression, as the drought came to be known, became the conservation crises of the century, and the conservation community mobilized to address the problem. Ding Darling, a newspaper reporter from the *Des Moines Register*, and Aldo Leopold were among the many people who called attention to the problem. At the urging of the conservation community, President Franklin D. Roosevelt called a national conference of hunters, conservationists, and politicians to address the plight of waterfowl.

As a university student searching for a project for my doctoral degree, I also attempted to work on this problem. I hoped to find support to do field research in the prairie pothole and aspen parklands regions of Canada, two of the most important nesting areas for waterfowl in North America, reportedly producing more than 75 percent of the ducks taken each year in the Central and Mississippi flyways.

One of the foremost research stations for wetland and waterfowl ecology was the Delta Waterfowl Research Station in Manitoba. It had earned great respect from conservationists everywhere for its contributions to wildlife science and management practices. Universities sent students there to do dissertation work, and many of today's waterfowl and wetland scientists and managers were trained at Delta. Located at the foot of Lake Manitoba and about twenty-five miles north of Portage la Prairie, the station is situated among the finest wetlands in North America, in the heart of the prairie parklands and deep-water lakes regions.

The area had been a favorite duck hunting marsh. Hunters from the United States and Canada had established lodges and camps at these wetlands. J. Ford Bell, chief executive officer of General Foods Corporation at the time, was one of these. Seeing waterfowl numbers decline in the drought years of the 1930s, Bell decided to conduct research and try to manage the waterfowl at Delta Marsh. He vowed to replace every duck he shot with ducks produced in a hatchery at the marsh edge and to sponsor research on the management and production of waterfowl.

He contacted Aldo Leopold of the University of Wisconsin and Miles Pirnie of Michigan State University about his plans, and together they started a research station at Delta. Leopold sent one of his promising graduate students, H. Albert Hochbaum, to begin research on the canvasback, numbers of which had declined to a point of deep concern. Hochbaum's classic *The Canvasback on a Prairie Marsh* was one of the first books issued from Delta, and the station soon expanded its interest to other species and other management efforts. Delta became a sort of proving ground for waterfowl biology and management, a place where government and private organizations met and explored the needs of waterfowl.

I wanted to be a part of this program. I contacted Bob McCabe at the University of Wisconsin, and he arranged an internship at Delta for me starting with the nesting season of 1954. He and Al Hochbaum, then the director at Delta, put me on a project to evaluate how predation by skunks, weasels, crows, and Franklin ground squirrels affected nesting success of pond ducks within the marshes of Lake Manitoba. I was elated. My work went well during the first nesting season, and I spent happy and productive hours in the marshes searching for duck nests, charting hatching and brood success and losses to predators.

On March 26, 1955, Joan and I got married in Mississippi, where we had met while I was teaching and she was going to school at Mississippi State College for Women (MSCW). We drove to Portage la Prairie. The frozen Assiniboine River was breaking up at almost the same hour as our arrival in the late afternoon of a cold April day. We bought supplies in town and then journeyed to Delta, where we established ourselves in a cabin furnished for us. The ground was frozen, and the first wash Joan hung out to dry froze stiff as a board. We cooked on a wood-burning iron stove, a real trial for newlyweds.

The Canadian prairies are among the most productive nesting habitats of waterfowl in North America. Unfortunately, ducks nesting in the prairie potholes and Aspen parklands are heavily preyed upon by birds and mammals. Over 70 percent of first nests of waterfowl are lost to crows, skunks, raccoons, Franklin ground squirrels, gulls, foxes and weasels. Second nesting attempts fared somewhat better. Predation was the major source of loss to nesting waterfowl. My project was to prevent predation and to assess its effects on production of ducks from this important habitat.

It was nesting study in which I attempted to assign causes and impacts of predation on duck production. Hochbaum and McCabe, my advisors, had dredged a large study area in the shape of a doughnut to prevent mammals from entering the protected area in the center of the dredged marsh. It could not exclude most mammals and certainly no predatory birds. During one of my visits to the Delta Waterfowl Research Station in the 1980s, thirty years later, the doughnut was barely visible.

I began my second year of field work with optimism and happiness. Then, as the nesting season of 1955 began, another side of life as a wildlife biologist began to express itself.

That year, wind tides from Lake Manitoba pushed water into my study areas and destroyed all the active duck nests along with the remaining nesting habitat. Most of the areas in and around Delta were inundated; even the little village of Delta was under water. It was a complete washout to say the least. I tried to pump out the marshes in my study area but with little or no effect. I kept the pump going 24 hours for several days, but water rushed in faster than I could pump it out. It was a disaster for me.

In some despair, I contacted Al Hochbaum and Bob McCabe. Both men sympathized but urged me to stay and continue the study. Regrettably, I decided to give it up, and Joan and I returned to Texas. It was a poor decision, and to this day I feel the incident was the worst of my career. In the intervening years, I've come to accept the failure but not the poor judgment of going against the advice of two outstanding scientists and educators.

Life as a university student was not as free as it had been in my youth on the San Gabriel. The adult world was an exciting place, but it came with a cost. I learned that diligence, persistence, and hard work were the principle keys to success, and I practiced them as best I could. I also learned that observation and the scientific method were the instruments of credibility. Nature had to be measured, analyzed, and described through numbers and usually through relationships with time, space, place, natural processes, and human interactions.

McCabe had enough faith to assign me to another project, on white-tailed deer in the Llano Basin of Texas, for which I received my doctorate. When I finally left university training, I had spent twelve years of study preparing for conservation work. I was recruited to the faculties of two universities, Mississippi State University and Texas A&M University, to teach and conduct research. After thirty years of work in higher education, in 1978, at age 52, I retired from Texas A&M University to become the director of the renowned Rob and Bessie Welder Wildlife Foundation near Sinton, Texas. In total, I worked without interruption in wildlife biology and conservation—the field for which I had trained—for fifty-five years of my lifespan. It is fair to say that, like a mat of algae floating on a pond, I was swept here and there by wind and luck as well as by solid training at major universities and an abiding love of the natural world.

FURTHER READING

Teer, James G. Controlled Waterfowl Hunting on a State-Owned Public Shooting Ground, Forney Lake, Iowa, 1950, *Iowa State College Journal of Science* 24, no. 5 (1952): 541–53. (MS thesis.)

Teer, James G., J. W. Thomas, and E. A. Walker. *Ecology and Management of White-tailed Deer in the Llano Basin of Texas.* Wildlife Monographs 15. Washington, D.C.: Wildlife Society, 1965. 62 pages. (Ph.D. dissertation.)

CHAPTER THREE

A Career and Life in Academia

A CAREER of protecting the natural world is a rewarding choice for young people with an interest in science and conservation. Yet, in the past, few high school seniors opted for university training in wildlife science. Although the field was expanding after World War II, it was still mostly unknown and little appreciated by students. Parents and counselors often advised students against conservation as a career choice. Today, however, many students are interested in the natural world and its protection.

Placement of graduates in conservation agencies and with private employers (non-government organizations and ranches) has increased as the field has grown. Enrollments have kept pace with the market and sometimes exceeded it. Young people now see conservation as a viable career choice, compatible with societal values that are imperative to the future of our nation and people. Our society has squandered the natural world in tradeoffs for material wealth and resources, often disregarding the fragility of nature and the uncertainty of its future. In the face of unending and often destructive demands on the environment for life's needs and comforts, conservation efforts often fail.

It is easy to become pessimistic about the continuing insults to the natural world and what they portend for the future of the planet. Yet an army of young people is studying for degrees in wildlife conservation and management in colleges and universities. The Wildlife Society, a professional organization in the United States, has more than eight thousand members, of whom about half are students. All have professional training and career interests in natural resources. Practically every state has a university with departments of wildlife and fisheries biology offering degrees that focus on conservation of wildlife and associated resources.

Wildlife conservation is much more than biology. A career in wildlife biology is daunting because of conflicting demands for natural resources by various users. Biological issues are most often expressions of things gone wrong. Management of nature usually seeks to correct human abuses to nature and, in many cases, to produce valuable goods and services for a growing human population. Social and economic dimensions are always part of the solutions to biological problems. Wildlife management could better be termed people management.

PROFESSORS IN THE TWENTY-FIRST CENTURY

Although I was not the best at it, my time as a professor in a major land grant university was an enjoyable and rewarding part of my life. I was always pleased to teach in the classroom and especially in the field; I enjoyed interactions with students and the subject matter. Lectures and laboratories that involved hands-on participation were the most rewarding of all.

The most successful teachers expose their students to the philosophical underpinnings, the technical subject matter, and the ecological processes involved in solving problems in conservation. But acceptance of the teacher and interest in the course were strongly related to how practical and applicable the material was. The relationship of the course to the realities of on-the-ground conservation was a major element both in the lecture hall and in the field.

Professor Robert R. Rhodes, a forestry professor, taught me in his field laboratory course that biological materials, processes, and phenomena could be measured and described in numerical values and currencies. Further, they must be measured to have validity in science. In each lab session, my classmates and I spent several hours measuring and describing vegetation in pastures grazed and ungrazed by livestock. Experiences in Rhodes's classes were a revelation to me. I admired him and adopted his field exercises because the techniques and subjects were similar to those I expected to use in future employment. As a student and ultimately a faculty member, I had similar learning experiences with other outstanding teachers. Practicality and relevance to real situations are important in the classroom.

Faculty positions are often divided between teaching, research, and public outreach and are structured to reflect these responsibilities. For example, duties may demand up to 90 percent of a person's time teaching and 10 percent on research, or the reverse may occur, with research being the major duty. Split appointments in teaching and research produce a broader and more effective teacher than one or the other alone.

I taught several courses over the years, at Mississippi State University (one year) and at three campuses in the Texas A&M University System (seventeen years at TAMU–College Station and one course each at TAMU–Kingsville and TAMU–Corpus Christi). The Texas A&M courses included Principles of Wildlife Management, Techniques in Wildlife Management, Conservation Biology, Population Dynamics, Community Ecology, and several seminars and special topics. In Mississippi I taught General Biology (Zoology and Botany), Comparative Anatomy, Aquatic Biology, and Wildlife Management. I usually taught one course each semester, even when serving as head of the department or in research projects conducted locally or abroad. And I learned more as a teacher than from any other activity I experienced on university faculties. Just about all aspects of university life come together there, and students are the pivot of it.

Unfortunately, universities do not reward teaching as well as they reward research and public service. They pay it lip service and may make attempts to improve teaching through seminars and workshops. But faculty members with productive research credentials are more eagerly sought and, more often than not, selected over good teachers. The number of research papers published and cited in prestigious, peer-reviewed journals is commonly emphasized in the selection of new hires. Search committees also give high marks to applicants with large dollar support obtained through grants and contracts. This kind of soft money can often be greater than the allocations from the state and university.

The tenure system, so revered and widely used by universities, has both good and bad qualities. It works to manage the best of us and often discards the worst among us, but it can be flawed in its practice and thus in its results. Some universities and colleges are discarding the tenure system as obsolete. Competition for resources and positions in academia is often fierce and sometimes abusive when gender, tenure, productivity, and conduct are considered. Most professors are bright, competitive, ambitious, and entrepreneurial. Political battles, jealousies, and disputes over resources, turf, and rank perhaps reach their acme in higher education. A department head once explained his duties to me like this: "My job is to protect the resources and turf of my department and to obtain the resources and turf of other departments!" Meant as a joke, his statement contained more than a measure of truth.

But are such values and conduct any different than those of business or any other human endeavor? I fear not.

THE CHANGING PROFILE OF STUDENTS

Students entering college to study wildlife biology today may have little prior knowledge of the field. For many, experience of nature derives largely from television and other mass media, with attendant anthropomorphizing and distortion. In decades past, lovable, humanized cartoon characters like Dumbo (1941) and Bambi (1942) had some unintended consequences: in my view, they turned public opinion against such management actions as reduction of deer and elephants in areas where reduction was the only reasonable alternative to die-offs from starvation.

Animated movies are a continuing influence. Now we have *The Lion King* and *Lion King II* (1994, 1998) and the penguins in *Happy Feet* (2006). Even when the cast of characters includes real animals—lions in *Born Free* (1966), great white sharks in *Jaws* (1975), or orcas in *Free Willy* (1993)—the reality of what is conveyed may be open to question. Growing up in urban settings as most of them do, and in the digital era, students usually lack firsthand knowledge of nature and awareness of conservation history. Although they know all the movies, they may never have encountered Aldo Leopold's thinking about our connections to the land.

The idea of conservation has also changed, as has students' perception of it. Recreational hunting has been declining for the past two or three decades, while non-consumptive uses of wildlife have increased. Wildlife biology, once largely confined to game animals, now emphasizes all species, huntable or not, and ecosystem management has replaced species management.

In the late 1960s and 1970s, students began demanding more relevance to reality in their courses than when I was an undergraduate. They became rebellious—more aggressive in their behavior and sometimes strident in their positions. Their reactions to subject matter heralded an awakening of independent thought that caught some professors off guard. Anyone who has bombed out in a lecture or speech knows how badly one's ego is damaged when the listener's interest flags.

I taught the introductory course Principles of Wildlife Management for most of my twenty-year teaching career at Texas A&M University, and it served as a sort of barometer for student thought about their studies. The course was (and is) popular because it gave freshman and sophomore students their first introduction to wildlife biology and management. Team taught by several professors, it regularly filled with a hundred or more students. At about the time of the first Earth Day in 1970, it changed somewhat to include environmental science. Air and water quality, the Farm Bill, and issues such as the ozone layer and global warming, endangered and threatened species, and community conservation became welcome additions to traditional topics in the course. Conservation and wildlife biology became more scientific and global, and the course was modified to reflect these trends and changes.

The last time I taught the course—in the late 1970s—the class filled with what seemed to me to be more mature and experienced students. During the first two or three lectures, I presented material that I had always presented as introductory precursors to traditional lectures. Species and habitat management and the governmental agencies responsible for managing issues and conflicts in conservation were major topics. At about the third lecture in the second week of the semester, I sensed discomfort in the class over these lectures.

Students did not usually express their displeasure at this early juncture in the course. Then a young woman approached and asked to speak with me after class. Timid she was not. She said, "Dr. Teer, I don't like this class and by your association with the course, I don't like you either. I enrolled to obtain information on endangered and threatened species. I want to spend my future in protecting them. Besides, the course is required for a baccalaureate degree in wildlife biology. Your lectures about agencies and organizations involved in conservation and about the history of conservation in the western world is dead material. We live in a world at risk of losing our natural resources and yet you burden us with irrelevant facts." Intense she was. "I enrolled in this major to save whales. You are wasting my time and that of the other students in this course." Teary eyed, she ended her discourse with, "We are dedicated and passionate about wildlife. Help us."

When I regained my composure some minutes later, I showed her the syllabus of the course. I advised her not to drop it (which I had already suggested). The syllabus and our discussion encouraged her, and she stuck with the course. By the end of the semester, she complimented me on it and even came to like me. Upon graduation she found employment with the International Whaling Commission, where she had a distinguished career. I am proud of her, and I learned a great lesson from this episode in the classroom.

Some students get discouraged and drop out or change majors after their freshman and sophomore years because of failing grades or required courses they consider peripheral and irrelevant to their future. Few equate university training in conservation and wildlife biology with courses in biology, chemistry, physics, calculus, and other difficult subjects. Further, the practice of wildlife conservation and management is not always pretty. The epic efforts of animals to survive predation, diseases, hunting, starvation, and other hardships are dramatically and truthfully depicted on TV and other mass media. Conflicts with humans for habitat are the biggest threat to wildlife, and societal values have not yet accepted the necessary costs of protection and preservation of habitat.

Notwithstanding the uncertainties and anxieties of university life, most students quickly grasp the expectations and demands of college. Completing the first two years with passing grades usually seals success in undergraduate studies. Every course is in some way relevant, even though information gained from them may never be used. If nothing else, they train young minds to think and to condition them for scientific deduction and analysis.

I have found that land grant universities are far and away better at preparing students for careers in wildlife and fisheries sciences than are liberal arts institutions. Unfortunately, students in some other universities where I have taught or have been privileged to review curricula and research are inadequately prepared in ecological sciences and wildlife management.

Some educators claim that current students are not interested in their studies and compare poorly with students enrolled in wildlife and fisheries sciences after Earth Day and during the environmental movement of the late 1960s and 1970s. Some blame the difference on outright apathy. Others say current students are made lazy by access to a world of knowledge on the Internet. At times, I have observed such differences, felt this way, and made such statements. I was wrong, and so are others who make them. With important exceptions, students in the twenty-first century are by and large brighter, more experienced, and broader in their range of knowledge than previous generations. Most students are learners if allowed to be. Their performance is hinged to the enthusiasm and knowledge of their professors. Poor teaching is often the cause of apathy. Skilled teachers are rare, and students are quick to recognize the good and the bad.

A STUDENT TO REMEMBER

By any measure, Jacobus du P. ("Koos") Bothma was the best student whose work I directed for an advanced degree. He came to the United States from South Africa to study for his doctorate at Texas A&M University. He had completed his baccalaureate and honors degrees at the

University of Pretoria. He had mastered most technical subjects in the research and socioeconomic dimensions of wildlife management.

My first contact with Koos was by mail, in a letter asking to study at Texas A&M. Theunis Steyn, the director of the Nature Conservation Branch of the Transvaal Province, and Dr. Fritz Eloff, chairman of the Department of Zoology at the University of Pretoria, realized that South Africa had few scientists with interests and expertise in wildlife ecology and management. Several of its universities had zoology departments; however, formal training in wildlife biology was not available in the country at the time. The lack of training centers in wildlife biology was a curious deficiency because wildlife resources were important among the economic and recreational resources in the nation.

Steyn and Eloff developed and funded plans to send one of their brightest students abroad for doctoral study. He was required to return to South Africa to staff and develop a wildlife research and teaching program at the University of Pretoria when he completed his studies. They estimated five years were necessary for Bothma to earn his degree. Hence he was sent to Texas A&M with full support for his subsistence and dissertation research during five years at the university and at the Rob and Bessie Welder Wildlife Refuge near Sinton, where he conducted the work. In total, the cost of Bothma's research project, fees, and subsistence was nearly sixty thousand dollars, most of which was provided by the South African government.

But Steyn and Eloff did not want to wait for Bothma to complete his studies. To get the wildlife program under way as soon as possible, they decided to bring to the university an American wildlife scientist for each of the five years. Starting in 1965 and continuing through 1969, American scientists from five major land grant universities were invited to participate, each teaching a nine-month honors course. The five professors were Dr. George Petrides of Michigan State University in 1965; Dr. Jim Jenkins of the University of Georgia in 1966; Dr. Ollie Hewitt of Cornell University in 1967; Dr. James Mumford of Purdue University in 1968; and I went from Texas A&M in 1969.

It was a grand plan and it worked without any serious problems. From ten to thirty students, primarily South Africans, registered for the course each year. Enrollment became progressively more cosmopolitan. In 2005, the annual enrollment, which is now capped at twenty students, comprised students from Europe, Asia, North America, and Africa.

Over the intervening years this program organized and developed by the three South Africans, Steyn, Eloff, and Bothma, evolved into the Center for Wildlife Management. The honors course remains the focal point of the center's teaching and research programs. The center became better known as South Africa emerged from its Apartheid years. Staff and students are now regularly asked by other African nations to conduct research and evaluate conservation needs. The center is a tremendous resource for conservation and has grown to several staff members, who do projects throughout Africa.

Koos Bothma was the very top degree candidate I supervised. He was a committed learner and the perfect student. He was as adept in field studies as he was in the laboratory. He accepted any challenge and worked as hard on cottontail rabbits as he did on the large, charismatic carnivores in which he specialized and which he continues to study. The author of seven books and numerous journal papers, Koos is now acclaimed as a great scientist and educator and a highly respected leader in conservation in Africa. His wife, Babsie, always works at his side.

TEACHING AND RESEARCH

Most of my career has been in academia as a professor and, in the latter stages, as an administrator or leader in university affairs. As a department head and principal investigator in research, I had responsibilities for major projects with multiple duties. These were pleasant though often difficult, and I was always proud of and satisfied with my assignments and positions. Working with students and gifted colleagues was a great experience. As most professors have observed, students are great teachers. I remember with pleasure and pride attending the bimonthly meetings of department heads in the College of Agriculture at Texas A&M. I sat with many whom I had known in my student life and also in the early part of my tenure as an assistant professor.

After spending a year as a lecturer in the Department of Zoology and Entomology at Mississippi State University (1953–54) and six years with the Texas Parks and Wildlife Department (1955–61), I became a faculty member of the Department of Wildlife and Fisheries Sciences at Texas A&M University in the fall of 1962. I replaced Dr. Charles O. Wallmo, who had left for a position with the U.S. Forest Service. Charlie was an outstanding scientist and teacher. He was one of those rare people whose demeanor and behavior always exuded competence, trust, and good will in his work and to his colleagues. Everyone liked him.

The department head at the time, Dr. William B. Davis, assigned to me the courses that Wallmo had taught: Techniques of Wildlife Management, and Principles of Wildlife Management. After several semesters I requested a new course, Population Dynamics. It was approved and became popular among both undergraduates and graduates. These were the courses designed for students interested in ecology and wildlife management.

I also inherited Charlie's research project on mule deer at the Black Gap Wildlife Management Area and Big Bend National Park in the Trans-Pecos region of Texas. The project's location was more than seven hundred miles from College Station. I spent considerable time traveling to and from the Trans-Pecos, living for days on the study area. It was beautiful desert and mountain country, and I enjoyed working there.

The density of mule deer on Black Gap had dropped precipitously, as it had throughout much of the western United States. Studies of the decline and the reasons for it became major field efforts. Further, population parameters and calculations of the composition of the herd were used in setting harvest quotas for a public hunt held each year in early December. While the region had a large mountain lion population, our field studies did not establish a serious predatory relationship between deer and lion numbers, even though we knew lions were regularly taking deer. Lions were important predators on a captive bighorn sheep herd on Black Gap, and a resident lion trapper, John McKinney, was stationed there to control lion numbers. (Plans to release bighorns did not materialize with this captive herd.)

It was on the Black Gap Wildlife Management Area that I used for the first time counts of deer pellet (feces) groups to arrive at the density of deer in particular habitats. Rain and insects were too destructive to the pellets for the method to work in the high rainfall areas of the United States. But the technique was widely used in the arid regions of the western states by deer biologists, and we preferred it in West Texas to other census techniques—aircraft, spotlight counts, and walking cruise counts. It was a simple method but yielded results roughly comparable to those from other deer census techniques.

To conduct the census, transects of known width and length, usually three feet wide and three hundred feet long, were swept clean of old pellet groups. To randomize the transect, an essential requirement of sampling design, the biologist threw a bicycle tire to locate the start of the transect. With knowledge of the defecation rates and number of new pellet groups deposited on the cleaned transects over a known period of time, the density and number of deer on the management area could be estimated.

More than once I had to explain to cowboys and others why we were flinging a bicycle tire around the pastures. Even more disconcerting to observers was the sight of someone sweeping the transects with a broom.

Most found the bicycle tire and broom extremely funny and were convinced beyond any doubt that biologists were daffy.

Settling in at a new position at Texas A&M University was difficult primarily because the university had few dollars for wildlife science. The department's operating budget was the lowest of the fifteen or so departments in the university's College of Agriculture. Lack of funds for his research was Charlie Wallmo's reason for leaving. Many conservation needs could not be addressed because there was no financial backing.

At that stage the department operated almost exclusively on grant and contract funds termed "soft money" by the university. Soft money was an apt name because it was unstable and was often used for fluff (unimportant purposes). Contracts and grants were difficult to obtain, and most were small amounts for specific projects. Research staff members and their students were expected to develop proposals and hustle for dollars to flesh out meager "seed money" provided by the Texas Agricultural Experiment Station, a part of the Texas A&M University System that also provided skeletal support for new hires.

My first project at Texas A&M (beyond Wallmo's mule deer study) was supported financially by four organizations with conservation interests. A grant of $1,500 was made by the Texas Agricultural Experiment Station for research on the reproductive habits of cottontails. Rabbits were considered agricultural pests and competitors with livestock for forage. They also supported an enormous number of hunters and thus were the number one mammal species in their bags. I could not have been more elated with the grant. At the time, $1,500 for wildlife research was not a bonanza, but it was sufficient to get the project going and it enabled me to leverage funding from other agencies.

When I compare the costs of doing research in 1965 to current costs, I am astounded at how little support we had. The cost of conducting comparable field research in 2008 is ten to fifteen times that in 1965, or more. Inflation is partly responsible, but funds are simply more available now than in the late 1960s. I am overwhelmed by the support that research now receives at Texas A&M. Grants and contracts of hundreds of thousands of dollars are not unusual. Several colleagues in the Department of Wildlife and Fisheries Sciences occupy endowed chairs and professorships paying more than $100,000 per year. Fringe benefits—that is, health care, retirement, and other perks—often add another $25,000 to a professor's salary. I understand the laments of older academicians when, like early professional sports figures, they compare salaries and equipment budgets of their times with those of the present.

As a teacher and administrator in a major wildlife and fisheries department, I was often called on to help review the wildlife research and teaching programs of other universities. I must have reviewed at least fifteen undergraduate and graduate curricula and operations. I was surprised at the similarity of the programs we reviewed, at how crowded curricula are in most degree programs, and at the small budgets that ran these operations.

In addition to being a team member of review committees, I assisted in developing teaching programs at the University of Pretoria in South Africa, the University of Moi near Eldoret, Kenya, the Aligarh Muslim University in India, and research programs at Nemours Wildlife Foundation in South Carolina, the Jones Foundation in Georgia, and the Welder Wildlife Foundation in Texas.

While I was the director of the Welder Wildlife Foundation, I joined three leaders in wildlife biology in the United States—Harry Hodgdon, executive director of the Wildlife Society; Jack Ward Thomas, chief of the U.S. Forest Service; and Oliver Torgerson, director of research at the Missouri Department of Conservation—in an attempt to answer the question "University Education in Wildlife Biology: What's Given and What's Needed?"

We were selected because we represented state and federal conservation agencies, non-government organizations, and private groups. It was a collegial assignment. Each of us had wrestled with the matter throughout our careers. Each felt he had won the battle of curriculum development for training students in basic science and conservation principles. We were surprised not by our differences but by how close we were to consensus on the major issues in university education in this field.

We presented the paper at the annual North American Wildlife and Natural Resources Conference. It was published in the proceedings of the conference and received wide attention in wildlife circles. Our summary statement in the paper was this:

> Wildlife conservation and management are more than biology. More often than not, conservation problems are solved not by biological information or scientific truth alone, but by a combination of considerations that sat-

isfy human needs and interests. Thus education in the field should include cross-over curricula between departments. These might include courses and emphases in habitat-oriented departments such as forestry, range management, agriculture, water resources, and marine science. Curricula should be flexible so that targets of students and needs of employers are accommodated. Economics, political science, public policy, sociology, conflict resolution, law, administration, and cultural anthropology especially in third-world nations are areas of value in natural resources conservation.

We believe it important that university wildlife programs have a complement of faculty members with experience in conservation agencies. With new diplomas and fresh from their own research experiences, new graduates are long in science but lacking in the application of it.

Salting and otherwise seasoning of faculties with veterans of the management "wars" would go a long way toward influencing students as to what is necessary in successful management careers.

Faculties of universities and colleges are among the most entrepreneurial organizations in American life and culture. Changes are being made through technology and scientific achievements that were unknown a few years ago. Universities continue to enhance their curricula and build their knowledge and programs on these changes. Administrators recognize that wildlife and fisheries are field and laboratory sciences with socio-economics and other human dimensions thrown in. The computer and other innovations created by science and technology can be enormous tools in conservation and management of the natural world but must be fed data from the field. Wildlife science is not a desk job. Unfortunately, emphasis on electronic gear can lead to training technocrats with little vision for human dimensions in conservation.

I am reminded of the fable in which several international students in genetic engineering produced a new tomato in the laboratory. It was a scientific breakthrough of international importance, much like the cloning of various animals, including white-tailed deer, domestic livestock, and pets. When the students with new diplomas and new tomato cultivars returned to their homes in separate lands, no one had been taught how to plant the new tomato. That is, even the most sophisticated science still needs basic underpinnings. For wildlife biologists, this means spending time in the field, asking appropriate questions, and avoiding redundancy. Technology can assist, but few solutions to problems in conservation are found in the office with a computer or calculator. The natural world is where the problems are and where they must be solved.

In my classrooms and during the course of my work in other countries, I found a great desire by young men and women to find employment abroad. International conservation attracts venturesome young biologists to work in exotic places on interesting species and their conservation. Many hope, as I did, to study and practice science abroad, to view the great wildlife spectacles of distant lands, and to help promote their conservation before they are wiped from the earth like my river, the San Gabriel. At one time or another, timidly and politely, students in most of my classes asked for information about how they might be employed in nature conservation in other lands.

Developing nations need the assistance of outsiders, who bring with them advances in technology and research and management tools and strategies. Most students who study abroad work with nothing more than a living wage for a few years, in the process gaining experience and viability in the job market back home. Few students gain full employment in other countries because they are usually interested in short-term assignments as they finish degrees. Further, conservation agencies in developing countries hesitate to employ outsiders, because they often publish the results of their work in scientific periodicals outside the nations where the work was done. In addition, some who wish to study abroad desire to do projects in their own particular interest areas rather than on topics that fit the needs of the employing agency.

To work abroad, one must establish credentials in international work, a difficult requirement at best. This may be a slow process of working in short-term projects with little pay. My suggestion to would-be international biologists has been and is to gain strengths in their own countries before attempting to market themselves in international work. The Peace Corps and non-government conservation organizations are excellent employment agencies for beginning conservationists. They can serve as good gauges for determining if applicants are really interested in working abroad, where cultural, social, and economic amenities may be vastly different from those at home. Some students cannot adjust. Nonetheless, despite the problems, the rewards are great.

WELDER WILDLIFE FOUNDATION

In 1978, at age fifty-two, I had been employed in academia for thirty years, the last nine at Texas A&M as head of the Department of Wildlife and Fisheries Sciences. During those years, I also held the Caesar Kleberg

Chair of Wildlife Ecology and Management. It carried with it heavy responsibilities for directing research mandated by the King Ranch to the Texas A&M University faculty.

While I had many opportunities for service to the causes of conservation and wildlife management, the responsibilities began to drag on me and I longed to return to more hands-on participation in research. As usually comes to academicians with proven records, I began to receive inquiries regarding employment at other universities and agencies, but I could not bring myself to leave Texas A&M even though I knew I was ready for something else in the field of conservation.

Two positions I hoped would come open someday were those of director and assistant director of the Rob and Bessie Welder Wildlife Foundation. Founded in 1954 by philanthropists Rob and Bessie Welder, the foundation supports education and research, primarily in South Texas, to enhance wildlife and its attendant economies. Foundation staff have been leaders in conservation affairs, and the organization has funded more than three hundred graduate students. The annual budget of the foundation, which operates as a 7,800-acre working cattle ranch, averages about $1.2 million. Its income is derived from oil, cattle, and, in some years, grants from other agencies.

I had a long history with the Welder Foundation. It had supported the writing up of my white-tailed deer research into my dissertation, and when I became a teacher I spent many happy hours there with my students. In 1974, the position of director came open with the retirement of Dr. Clarence Cottam, the foundation's first director. Cottam, who was my friend, called to see if I might be interested. He invited me to meet with him, his assistant W. C. Glazener, and three trustees of the foundation, M. Harvey Weil, John J. Welder IV, and Patrick H. Welder. I readily accepted their invitation and spent more than a day reviewing the foundation's programs and finances and the duties of the director. To no one's surprise, I learned that the foundation operated with rock solid goals and financial support.

But on that occasion I turned the position down simply because Texas A&M University remained closer to my heart and soul. Glazener became director and remained in the position for four years. In 1978, he called to tell me he was retiring and asked if I would be a candidate again. This time, I accepted. For Joan and me, living and working on a cattle ranch surrounded by untrammeled nature was a highlight of our life together. The foundation's land was home to animals of all kinds, including a great deer herd, the Rio Grande turkey, javelina, waterfowl of all kinds, and more than 350 species of songbirds.

Nothing that I can set down in these pages can overstate the value of private foundations in conservation issues, nor the pleasure and satisfaction in working with them. They seem to be able to avoid much of the rancor that often forms around heated public discourse over the use and management of natural resources. Foundations and research stations are now becoming more numerous and active in conservation affairs. I am proud to have participated in the development of the conservation programs of four foundations, all highly beneficial. Besides the 7,800-acre Rob and Bessie Welder Wildlife Foundation near Sinton, Texas, they are the 26,000-acre Jones Foundation in southern Georgia, the 12,000-acre Nemours Wildlife Foundation in South Carolina, and the 6,000-acre Theodore Roosevelt Ranch in Montana.

I retired as the foundation's director in 1998 after twenty years. Texas A&M University named me professor emeritus, and Joan and I moved back to College Station. At this writing, I have an office in the Department of Wildlife and Fisheries Sciences at Texas A&M University.

WILDLIFE CONSULTANCIES ON TEXAS RANCHES

Field biology is an inexact science. Wildlife biologists do not wear the clean white coats of laboratory scientists and physicians. Rather, most wear jeans, boots, and sometimes a wide-brimmed hat but usually a baseball cap with someone's advertising on it. Although technology and scientific techniques for studying and managing wildlife have improved greatly in recent times, the basis for wildlife and habitat management remains work in the field.

For more than thirty years, I served as a wildlife management consultant to several cattle ranches in Texas. I was usually asked to census deer from helicopters. From these surveys, I calculated harvest quotas for upcoming hunting seasons. In addition, I advised landowners on habitat and hunter management for both deer and bobwhite quail. Texas A&M University and the Rob and Bessie Welder Wildlife Foundation permitted outside consulting, which I did on weekends and vacations. Whenever I asked my employers for permission to serve as a consultant, I was cautioned not to forget who paid my salary.

I consulted on several large ranches for ten years or more, on one for fifteen years, and on another for twenty-two years. All were in the Rio Grande Plains of Texas and noted for their trophy deer. Among them were the Chaparrosa (ca 67,000 acres) and Mangum (ca 10,000 acres) ranches, owned by Belton Kleberg Johnson; Hacienda Campo Alegre (ca 6,000 acres), owned by Nelson and Mark Rockefeller; Green Lake (ca 25,000 acres) and the San Patricio ranches (ca 6,000 acres), owned by Patrick H. Welder; and the Apache, Crooked River, La Copa, and Encino divisions of the King Ranch, operated as hunting leases by Dresser Industries, an oil well drilling and service company with offices worldwide and John Blocker as vice president.

Hunting leases were used to entertain clients and persuade them to buy oil drilling and production equipment and other products. Corporations and professional groups chose hunting and outdoor activities over more routine kinds of business entertainment, such as weekend visits to Hawaii or Las Vegas, golfing and other sports events, or theater tickets to Broadway shows. Corporate leaseholders believe that taking people out hunting and fishing produces more sales than traditional entertainment activities do. Competition among companies for the better game ranges caused lease prices to escalate to levels that priced many individuals out of the market for hunting. The resulting high costs remain a major problem in the state's efforts to provide equitable opportunities for all its citizens to hunt and fish. The decline over time in the number of hunters and license sales is due in part to the high price of access to wildlife.

Conducting censuses of deer to assess herd dynamics in South and Central Texas was my main activity as a consultant, but the accuracy of helicopter censuses has always been contested. Nick Morris, leaseholder of the 22,000-acre Welder Heirs Ranch in southwest Texas, a friend and my client for a short period, complained that no two biologists thought alike about deer numbers. Nick's observation reflects the fact that most biologists recommended conservative harvest rates to prevent overharvest, and some use "fudge factors" to adjust for deer not seen on the transects. Charles de Young, a gifted biologist at the Caesar Kleberg Wildlife Research Institute, determined from marked deer that up to 50 percent of deer on aerial transects were not seen.

Surveys of wildlife are difficult at best and nearly impossible in some terrain and vegetation. To control some of the vagaries of aerial census work, standardization was necessary. Weather, visibility, time (of day and season), speed and height of the aircraft, use of the same observers and pilots, and even stages of the moon were considered in census efforts. With careful adherence to consideration of these variables, census results varied within about 20 percent from one count to the next, but replication and standardization of conditions were never sufficient to keep variances to low levels.

I usually supplemented aerial counts with field surveys of the herd's composition. Sex, age, antler development, body size, physical condition of the deer, and the quality of their range were usually ciphered into estimates of numbers of deer to be taken. Night counts on road transects were sometimes conducted to see how aerial counts compared. The science went as far as the data permitted; however, art and experience took over at some point in the calculations.

Consideration of the goals on a given ranch also figured into the estimates. Some ranches managed deer for trophy quality; others managed for the number of bucks of all age classes and antler development. Recommendations for removing antlerless deer usually involved numbers more than twice those for bucks, because bucks have a higher natural mortality rate than females and most ranchers overharvest the buck segment of their herds.

Precision of deer counts was notably enhanced when they were made on the same transects in early fall year after year. October through early November was the usual time selected for censuses. Long-term trends in numbers were established over several years, which reflected the cumulative status of the herd. When aerial censuses and ground surveys agreed, confidence in the estimates rose. Seldom did I experience an aberrant census so great that it was unusable.

Most wildlife biologists use the principle of adaptive management in the management of a deer herd and range. This meant adjusting harvest quotas to meet changes in conditions as a result of perturbations such as drought, heavy predation on fawns, or overharvesting of the herd. It was a matter of constantly assessing the herd and the range that supported it. When data were obviously incorrect or mistakes were made in our harvest recommendations, I took some comfort in the knowledge that white-tailed deer have a high reproductive rate and are responsive to overharvest. With twins the general rule for adult deer and with a polygynous mating system, deer respond to overharvesting by increasing fawn production. They soon return to former numbers.

To census bobwhite and other quail, call counts are made on preestablished transects in the spring, in which the number of calls are counted and compared to previous counts. Quail productivity is exceptionally responsive to weather, primarily rainfall. Counts of calling quail and observations of quail pairs, broods, and coveys are numerical values that can predict the quality of quail hunting in the fall and winter hunting seasons.

Consultants are often employed to meet requirements of the government to protect sensitive and endangered species. I was employed on several occasions to prevent habitat degradation by oil field activities. Pipeline construction, oil spills, leaks from tank batteries and vehicles that transport oil to refineries, 3D seismograph operations, and other activities of the industry have major impacts on wildlife habitat. Environmental impact statements must usually precede any disruptions of habitat used by endangered and threatened species. Endangered species are protected by the Endangered Species Act of 1973 and other legislation. Government agencies often contract with private consultants to develop recovery plans and to protect species from land use practices that destroy their habitat and put them at risk.

Working as a consultant on ranches that had different goals and motivations for enhancing wildlife provided me with learning experiences that could not be obtained in the classroom. It laced my academic life with real world experiences and helped me address the vagaries and inconsistencies of biological data and the results emerging. Experiences gained in managing wildlife on ranches prepared me for teaching, which in turn helped me prepare students for meeting the problems and possibilities of wildlife-related land uses in Texas. Aside from the merit of expanding my management experience, consulting was fun and interesting. I encourage students to seek internships or summer employment with conservation agencies and wildlife ranches so as to experience and understand the rigor of field work and how crucial it is for the successful management of wildlife.

FURTHER READING

Teer, James G. Educating Resource Managers for the Future. Will Forestry Educators Meet the Challenge? Society of American Foresters Annual Meeting, Denver, Colo., 1991. 8 pages.

Teer, James G., H. D. Hodgdon, J. W. Thomas, and O. Torgerson. University Education: What's Given and What's Needed. *Transactions, 55th North American Wildlife and Natural Resources Conference* (1990):126–32.

CHAPTER FOUR

People and Conservation

MY EXPERIENCES with people and conservation and the human spirit are the most interesting and coveted memories in my life's journey. I have now also placed them at the top of my pleasure list in writing about them. Each account reawakened acquaintances and renewed my awareness of the people with whom I worked—people with interesting lives that were shaped by their particular settings and their contributions to wildlife conservation.

Obviously, I could not include all those who influenced or assisted me. To satisfy the sins of omission, I have selected people who were important in my youth, during college, and ultimately in my career. I have avoided writing about my family, although when all is weighed, family members were the most important in every endeavor; without them, none of it would have been possible.

EARLY MENTORS

In almost every place I worked in conservation, a man of advanced age was there to assist and teach me. This was not planned or ordered by my employers or professors nor solicited by me. Their presence just seemed to happen. Three of these old men were special, and I established a friendship with one of them before I had any thought of a career in natural science.

In my youth, there was A. S. Hall, in Granger, Texas, where I was born and lived through my teen years. Mr. Hall was a gentle man who lived his life in the natural world and made his living from it.

At Forney Lake in Freemont County in southwest Iowa, where I spent seven months conducting graduate research, there was Silas Thompson. Mr. Thompson had a small boat livery at the marsh's edge, renting out boats to cane pole fishermen in the warm seasons and to duck hunters in the fall and winter. The lake had excellent fishing for mud cats, and Iowans seemed to prefer them to other game species.

Back in Texas, at the Engeling Wildlife Management Area, there was George Crist. Mr. Crist was employed by the State of Texas for his intimate knowledge of the area. I met him when I took a job as a biologist at the Engeling WMA.

Each was like a page that, once read, was turned so that the next page opened. Each was in his seventies when I knew him. By all standards except that of intimate knowledge of nature, each would be considered poor. They lived on the edge and managed to wrest a meager living from the natural world. I was attracted to them not because they were old, poor, wise, or pleasant but because they lived the kind of life to which I aspired. They knew the wild world not through books but by personal experiences. I always used "Mister" in addressing them: Mr. Hall, Mr. Thompson, and Mr. Crist.

Each of these old men befriended me and offered experiences that no others could produce. I suppose each also served me as a surrogate for the father who had left us. During the bad times and the good, I think back to their lives and find pride and example in their friendship. They hold special places in my recollections as mentors in the best definition of the word.

A. S. Hall

The mentor of my early youth was the kindly A. S. Hall, truly a man of nature. He was uneducated but bursting with knowledge gained directly from the natural world. He more or less adopted me and supplied a learning experience not available in books.

Mr. Hall made his living from nature. During winter months, he hunted cottontail and swamp rabbits in the bottomlands by "shining" them with carbide or battery-powered miners' lamps attached to his hat. He usually took fifteen to twenty rabbits during each outing. Most were sold to black people in Austin and on the "flat," the term given to the Negro section of Granger. He peddled his kills for up to a dollar apiece. He also sold wood cut in the bottomlands and sawed it in lengths and split it into sizes to fit in wood stoves and fireplaces. His saw was powered by an ingenious coupling with belts to one of the back wheels of his Model T truck.

During the warm seasons of the year, Mr. Hall fished the creeks and rivers for catfish, which he sold to customers in Granger and elsewhere. He fished the dens and holes in stream banks where channel, flathead, and blue catfish nested. He used a long, keen cedar pole, twenty feet or more, to which was attached a set of treble hooks wrapped in a bright piece of cloth. By teasing the fish with the pole, he would soon provoke them to attack it and be hooked. At this point, Mr. Hall would unwind a long cord attached to the treble hook and wound around the pole. He pulled the fish out of its den and onto a nearby gravel bar or into shallow water.

Although it was illegal, "noodling" was widely used in the southern United States. He was enormously successful. He learned the location and sizes of commonly used dens and visited these as a trapper might visit his sets. Mr. Hall commonly caught two or three large fish weighing between twenty and fifty pounds on each trip to their "holes."

I accompanied him as often as I could or as often as he would take me. On one memorable occasion, he came near to harm when he caught a large blue catfish in a bank underneath a large pecan tree overhanging the river. The fish, weighing more than eighty pounds, responded to his

A. S. Hall, a mentor during my early years in Granger, with his daughter and huge catfish caught in the San Saba by "noodling." Hall made his living as an outdoorsman and taught me a good deal about nature.

teasing. It began to buck and fight the colored hooks. I had climbed the pecan tree and positioned myself in the overhanging limbs where I could feel the fish's bucking and fighting.

The big fish took the hooks but refused to leave its den. To get a better hold of the cord attached to the hooks, Mr. Hall went underwater and into the mouth of the den to try to get the quarry out. It seemed a very long time before he surfaced with the cord and fish. The fish pulled Mr. Hall, who weighed about 140 pounds, out into and down the stream for about fifty yards. He wrestled it finally onto a gravel bar where it was subdued.

Fishing with this technique was somewhat dangerous, but when Mr. Hall did it he was careful about the size of the fish. Flathead and blue catfish reached more than eighty pounds and were a match for a small man. He often thrust his hand into the fish's mouth and grasped its gills. Catfish have teeth in both the upper and lower jaws. They are much like a set of wire bristles that, when sawed back and forth by a mad fish, caused severe abrasions to the fisherman's arm.

Because his fishing technique was illegal, Mr. Hall always took the back roads and traversed sparsely inhabited areas of Central Texas to reach and fish his streams. His Model T truck was slow but dependable, and as far as I know, he was never stopped by a game warden. I enjoyed the cat and mouse game, as if we were back in a farmer's watermelon patch, but Mr. Hall did not.

He asked me to come by his house on the day I took the bus to San Antonio in June 1944 to enter the U.S. Navy. Mrs. Hall put together a bag of sandwiches and fruit for me to take on the three-day train trip to boot camp in San Diego. Mr. Hall did not write to me during my fifteen-month absence in the Pacific. I'm not sure if he was literate. Occasionally he sent me a sack of native pecans gathered in the San Gabriel River bottomlands. When I was discharged, we resumed our friendship until I left for college in September 1946. I saw him infrequently after this. He was by then a very old man and not as active in hunting and fishing as he had once been, and I had gone on to other things.

Silas Thompson

When Edward Kozicky stationed me on Forney Lake in Iowa to conduct my master's research, I was the only resident on the lake except for Silas Thompson and a few farmers on adjacent land, including Frank Forney, for whom the lake was named.

Mr. Thompson operated a small boat livery of no more than three homemade wooden skiffs. He rented them to fishermen and hunters who visited the marsh. In appearance and especially his mannerisms, he reminded me of Andy Clyde, a movie comedian often seen, if you had a dime, on short subjects at Saturday morning movies. With glasses low on his nose, uncombed hair under a straw hat in the warm season or a felt hat in the cold, he usually sported a week's beard. His blue and gray striped bib overalls appeared a bit unwashed.

Mr. Thompson was the epitome of a man of complete independence from the responsibilities of marriage, position, and other societal obligations. He appeared comfortable in his lifestyle and happy with what life had dealt him—a tonic to those of us who were harnessed in various ways to people and jobs. He waited for me on his dock. At dusk, after I had spent a cold day on the marsh with my ducks, he often met me with coffee as hot as the stove and as strong as the stew pan in which it was boiled and from which the grounds were strained through one's teeth. As often as not, he invited me to supper. He taught me much about the natural history of the marsh and its inhabitants, details that could not be found in books or classrooms. He was a treasure trove of nature lore and fact.

Forney Lake was an ox-bow lake formed by the meanderings of the Missouri River. It was a cattail/bulrush marsh of several hundred acres. Like all such waters, it was rich in the requirements for life and was a favorite fishing hole for Iowans in spring and summer and for duck hunting in the fall. Most fishermen used a cane pole. They seemed to prefer bullhead catfish, the lesser cousins of such game fish as bass, bluegills, and crappie. Fishing on Forney Lake was the kind of fishing one can enjoy on a warm, sunny afternoon, watching a bobber and spending little energy in landing yellow and brown bullheads. It seemed to fit Iowans, they had discovered the simple pleasures.

Mr. Thompson developed a cancerous growth on his neck late one fall. During his illness, he remained in his shack at the marsh, operated his livery, and received minimal treatment. He succumbed to the cancer at about the time the marsh froze in December. His friend Tommy Tucker, with whom he had spent many happy hours playing low- or no-stakes poker and visiting, arranged his funeral. I never knew if he had a family.

I have visited southern Iowa in recent years, but the marsh is not there. Forney Lake has been drained and converted to farm land; an exchange I consider a poor trade resulting in net loss to the region. About the only features suggesting it was once a marsh are the ridges and berms pushed up by the ice along the former shoreline and the channels through which the water was drained. All else is gone except vast cornfields. It would have been better for me not to have returned. We have more corn because of its demise. We have less of the life that gentles us and stirs our souls.

George Crist

I first met Mr. Crist at the Engeling Wildlife Management Area near Palestine, Texas, in 1952. Because of his detailed knowledge of the area's natural and legal history, he was employed at age seventy-two on the 10,960-acre refuge. Mr. Crist and his wife, Della, had been married for more than fifty years by the time I met them. The Texas Game, Fish and Oyster Commission purchased the old Derden Ranch, 5,500 acres near Tennessee Colony in Anderson County. It was one of the last relatively undisturbed large parcels of land remaining in the post oak vegetation zone in East Texas. It was open range and was used vigorously by everyone. Neighbors used it for grazing their livestock and fattening their hogs on the abundant acorns and for picking berries for the jams and jellies they made. Wildlife was plentiful—deer, squirrels, waterfowl, and turkeys. The local people used the area as their own.

Mr. Crist was born on the property and knew every detail. He could show you stakes put up by surveyors more than seventy-five years previously, when he worked as a cowboy for the Derden family. He could outline the drainage patterns that emptied into Catfish Creek, and as was ultimately required, he could lay out roads for access and erect fencing to control the livestock released on the property. He was a natural historian. He knew every plant, animal, ecological system, and habitat for wildlife. His names were often more descriptive than scientific, with special meanings gained by experienced interactions with them.

Mr. Crist was a valuable asset to the development of the Engeling area and a bonus in my work as a biologist on the refuge. We worked together on many projects. Our immediate boss was John M. Carlisle, who knew how to supervise men and their work. But work on the refuge did not start well because a terrible tragedy occurred just as I was to join the project.

When I completed my master's degree at Iowa State University in December 1951, I applied for a biologist's position with the Texas Game, Fish and Oyster Commission. W. C. Glazener, then director of the Wildlife Restoration Division, hired me to begin work on January 1, 1952. I was to be assistant to Gus Engeling, the refuge manager. My brother Donald drove to Ames to pick me up. I was elated at prospects for my future.

When I arrived home in Texas a few days before Christmas, on December 20 to be exact, I learned from friends that Gus Engeling had been murdered by a poacher on the refuge on December 13. His murderer was at that moment being sought. I could see my job evaporating before I had a chance to fill it.

Gus was killed while investigating gunshots that had put up large skeins of ducks from Catfish Marsh. He had been in the vicinity to investigate an oil spill being repaired by a work crew. On hearing shots and seeing the ducks, he went to investigate. When another shot was heard and Gus did not return to the pipeline, the crew became worried. A search for him was started. He was not found for several days because the marsh was frozen over with skim ice. Then one of the searchers caught a glimpse of a shiny object in the water: an eyelet on Gus's boot. He had been shot with a shotgun at close range and had died immediately. The murderer had stuffed his body under logs in the marsh

The sheriff and his men investigated the murder and, to everyone's surprise, found a pair of glasses at the scene. Several people identified the man who wore them. Alton Parish, a man with a large family known for poaching, was questioned and admitted to the crime. He usually sold his kills to local people in Palestine, a small town some thirty miles from the refuge. Like many in the area, Parish considered the unposted refuge free range on which hunting, grazing, and fishing were open to the public.

After the murderer was apprehended and jailed, Glazener called me to report to the Engeling refuge at once. I drove a Dodge Power Wagon to the refuge. The murderer's adult sons had vowed and bragged that they would send some of the "state men" with their father when he was punished for his crime. Within a year Parish was tried, convicted, and sentenced to die in the electric chair. Glazener asked John Carlisle to suggest ways for us to protect ourselves. We were required to wear firearms for several months and always to work in pairs. Even with these requirements, I was happy to have a job in the field for which I had trained. It was a great pleasure to work with staff and leaders in the Texas Game, Fish and Oyster Commission's wildlife restoration program. Mr. Crist worked with me during these troubled times, without any confrontations or problems with the Parish family.

I soon learned from him that traditions and restrictions applied to resources found "in the woods." A bee tree with an "X" carved in its bark belonged to the person who had marked it. It was to be left for the person who had discovered it, to be cut at his convenience. Free-ranging livestock with ears clipped at strategic places was not free to everyone. To take a marked animal was hateful and, if discovered, the taker was sure to be subject to retribution. Those of us working for the state were circumspect in our conduct and interactions with the local people. Even so, several months elapsed before they accepted us. Their acceptance was partially due to our respect for their traditions.

Mr. Crist befriended me in my work and in my personal life. He kept my bird dogs, and Della always had food for me. Once, two of my bird dogs escaped their pens and killed almost thirty of the Crists' chickens. I can never forget the pain on their faces as we drove into their yard and saw dead chickens strewn throughout. And I cannot forget my pain in knowing I was the cause. I replaced the chickens but always knew that the Crists would have preferred to have their own birds.

I worked at the Engeling refuge for almost two years. The biology and management of deer, turkeys, quail, and their habitats held many lessons to be learned. This job in conservation was the first I had on graduating from college. The Crists were a major part of it.

The friendship and mentoring of Mr. Hall, Mr. Thompson, and Mr. Crist were important to my growing understanding of nature. They were as important in shaping my future as any university professor. I learned from them that knowledge and wisdom are not the property of any select group and that friendship and good will are the first ingredients of success.

MY HEROES

The contributions of some individuals to conservation of wildlife have been of heroic proportions, literally changing societal values and mores. Theodore Roosevelt, Gifford Pinchot, C. Hart Merriam, George Bird Grinnell, and Aldo Leopold quickly come to mind, and there is no shortage of other leading figures in the development of conservation ethics and practices. Fellow conservationists have not labeled these people with the word *hero*, and I suspect few students could name two of the five mentioned or describe the historic contributions they made. Nonetheless, they were important voices in our history when we had decimated a series of species through profligacy, greed, and a comfortable belief that wildlife was inexhaustible.

Most conservationists spend a lifetime toiling in the trenches of wildlife management with little or no recognition of their work. Add those who do hit a professional home run in science or management, however, and the sum total of their collective contributions has had lasting effects on issues that vex and challenge the world. Given time, some will be cited for their work in one way or another. Recognition of achievements is important in fields where the results may come in small increments and take time to be tested and accepted. As one friend declared, "Biologists seldom look behind themselves and when they do, they cannot see the ditch they've dug"—there always remains so much still to do.

Throughout my career, I have been fortunate to have had colleagues who also became close friends. Biologists at universities, state and federal agencies, and non-government organizations were sources not only of expert information but also of good company. Early on, I sought to become acquainted with leaders in wildlife science and to study their work. If I did not meet them at professional meetings, I learned about them through their publications. By the time I had finished my graduate degrees, I had developed a knowledge of the conservation community, its history, and its leaders. Meeting some of these people face to face was an unexpected pleasure and proved invaluable to my studies and employment opportunities.

The first and only North American Wildlife and Natural Resources Conference that I attended as an undergraduate student was held in San Francisco in 1949. Six student colleagues and I drove to the conference in a van, three days each way. After graduation I rarely missed this annual meeting. The "North American" remains a valuable meeting, which I have missed only two or three times since 1949. The annual meetings of the Wildlife Society, American Ornithologists' Union, and Society for American Mammalogists were three others that I attended each year. All were gatherings of people dedicated to advancing the management of natural resources, and several of those people would become mentors and close friends to me.

Lee M. Talbot

One man who has served as a model for me is Lee M. Talbot. He has been my hero for many years for his contributions to conservation through research, administration, and public service. I have never expressed this to him, I suppose because men often don't convey such admiration and respect.

Having graduated from the University of California at Berkeley in geography, and grandson of the famous ecologist C. Hart Merriam, Lee has worked for more than five decades in global conservation. He is a quiet man, which some wrongly interpret as aloofness or even coldness, but Lee is a helpful and cooperative professional with a friendly and warm personality. And it would be a serious mistake not to acknowledge his wife, Marti, as a major participant in his work; she, as much as Lee, deserves the term *hero*.

Lee and Marti Talbot, two of the great leaders in conservation in the twentieth century, were among the very first to study the great Serengeti ecosystem. Here they measure blue wildebeest, which now number nearly two million animals. Lee's contacts in the world conservation community were essential to studies of releases of nonnative big game species into Texas and elsewhere in the United States. Photo courtesy of Lee Talbot.

Lee's contributions have been "firsts." Projects on other continents give an idea of the breadth and importance of his life. He was a field research biologist for a good part of his career and was among the first scientist-conservationists with international interests. One of his early assignments was in southern Asia and the Middle East in the mid-1950s, to determine the status of several large mammals that were at risk of extinction. Sent by Harold J. Coolidge, vice president of the International Union for the Conservation of Nature (IUCN), Lee obtained first-hand knowledge of seven endangered species: the Asian lion in India's Gir Forest and the Kashmir stag in northern India; the Arabian oryx and Syrian wild ass in the Middle East; and the Indian, Sumatran, and Javan rhinoceros. His field studies were important in establishing IUCN as a global voice in conservation.

Many years later, Lee was a principal in organizing a project to raise Arabian oryx in captivity for restocking the ranges in the Middle East from which they had been extirpated. He was a major force in obtaining a captive herd of oryx from zoos and private stocks to establish a breeding colony of the species in Phoenix, Arizona. The project was successful after several years, and most of the animals were sent to the Middle East to establish breeding colonies in Jordan, Saudi Arabia, and Syria. Oryx produced in those colonies were then re-introduced into suitable habitats.

At a meeting of IUCN in Amman, Jordan, in 1999, conference authorities organized a field trip to visit the breeding colony outside Amman. Around 140 oryx were kept at the station, most of which had been born there. Lee, Marti, and I viewed the animals, talked with their keepers, and learned about their restocking program. Lee and Marti showed unabashed pride in the project. Their faces radiated sheer enjoyment. Characteristically, both tried to divert any praise of their role in the success of the project to others.

Wildlife credentials aside, I was surprised to learn that Lee is an accomplished race car driver. He has assembled a team of his sons and several friends and has raced competitively for many years. He has excelled in this activity as he has in conservation science. One would suspect his longevity has been tested in both pursuits.

Jack Ward Thomas

As a project leader with the Texas Game and Fish Commission in 1956, I hired Jack Ward Thomas—then just out of college—to work on a deer survey project in the Edwards Plateau and the Llano uplift region of Texas. Jack reported to our camp early one afternoon in September 1957, before we scattered to conduct a late afternoon deer cruise count. The six-man crew met him and tried to make him welcome. He was immediately inspected by Emmit Smith, one of the older hands with long experience as a deer trapper for our project. Emmit was always suspicious of new recruits. He rejected everyone. On the surface, they just didn't measure up to what Emmit wanted them to be. He detected no sign of the distinction Jack would later achieve.

Emmit took me aside and said, "Jim, this guy ain't gonna make it. Did you see his dress: low-top slippers and cotton pants and short-sleeve shirt? He'll get torn up here in this thorn bush or he'll get snake bit before dark today. I'll bet he can't tell a mesquite tree from a live oak. We'll have nursed him along for some time before he contributes anything to our work. Why don't you send him packing?"

I had heard Emmit's appraisals of new hires before. It happened every time a new person joined our crew. I assured him that Jack would do fine if we made a place for him in our work. We did, and Jack became a leader in our field studies and ultimately a national figure in conservation. He replaced me as project leader when I left to continue studies for my doctorate at the University of Wisconsin in Madison. Jack remained in Llano for several years before he left to study for his own doctorate at the University of Massachusetts.

For Jack, one rite of passage in learning his position was to work a hunter check station. We had him and two technicians manning a deer check station near Hondo, Texas. They operated the check station for six weeks without relief. The technicians resigned a number of times, sometimes twice a day, and attempted to hitchhike home to Sonora. Jack was unmoved at their pleas; with humor, good will, and empty promises of relief within a few days, he finally persuaded them to remain on the job.

After completing our deer surveys, we issued antlerless permits to ranchers who wanted to reduce the number of deer on their ranches. Jack set up an "office" consisting of an apple box at the check station and issued permits as ranchers stopped by to request them. Mr. "Good Eye" Haby stopped to request permits to take several deer from his property. Jack issued them to him on the basis of our deer surveys. Along with the permits, Jack also gave each rancher a drawing of a deer's uterus and ovaries, which we wanted people to collect for our studies of deer reproduction. We made a careful illustration of the reproductive tract, depicted in the opened abdominal cavity of a deer lying on its back, so that the rancher would know how to position the deer to find and remove what we wanted.

Jack showed Haby the drawing and requested that he cut out the tract and place it in the bag provided for the purpose. Haby didn't quite understand the process. "Mr. Thomas, if I don't have a pair of scissors to remove the picture, can I use my pocket knife?" he asked. Careful explanation was required for Haby to understand what in the world we wanted and why, and he eventually contributed several tracts to our studies. We collected more than 3,500 reproductive tracts, which were used in a major part of my thesis research.

We didn't always receive what we had requested. Kidneys, testes, and other parts were turned in at the check stations where the hunters were required to register their kill of deer.

Jack is a great storyteller and used his humor and good will to calm waters even in the most turbulent storms, of which there were many in his professional life. After many prestigious assignments and positions, he was appointed chief of the U.S. Forest Service, not an easy appointment for a wildlife scientist. Foresters accepted Jack's leadership, some with great reluctance and others with the view that Jack would and could change the "timber beast." His tenure as chief of the Forest Service brought important changes. After three years, he left to become the Boone and Crockett Professor at the University of Montana, where he delighted in classroom teaching.

I follow Jack's career with special interest, and he remains a close friend although he resides in Montana and I in Texas. I have long boasted shamelessly about giving him his first job in conservation, so that the renown he has earned will reflect on me. Fifty years after our first meeting in our camp on the Llano River, I still brag, "Yeah, I hired Jack Thomas when he was a fledgling." We recall the good times and troubles of our youth—finances, marriages, and work—and I count hiring him as among my more important contributions to wildlife. Our nostalgic greeting today is, "It's a long way to Llano."

THE UNHOLY FIVE

Until the third millennium raced into my life, I was a member of a group of men bound together by love of hunting and the outdoors. The group did not come about by calculation or design; it slowly evolved over the years. Our backgrounds and common interests fueled the start and guided its composition. Belonging to this group was a highlight of my life and lasted more than thirty years, until the passing of three of the five members.

There was nothing unique about our group. Because hunting is more than killing animals, people do not ordinarily wish to hunt and camp alone. Most often, hunting parties consist of men with like interests and values. Candidates for membership may wait years for a vacancy into one party or another, or they may never be accepted. The system is not unlike what drives some country clubs or fraternities, with rules of conduct and hunting interests more important than position or status in society.

The five men in our group had deep similarities. Our commonalities were rooted in our love of the natural world and of hunting game birds and big game. Hunting was the attractant that collected us. Friendship cemented us together. We spent many happy hours in camps near windmills where we could get water or bathe in a horse trough. Or we simply didn't bathe. Mostly we hunted quail. On occasion we killed a deer for camp meat or for taking home to our families. It is difficult to take oneself seriously at play, and play it was. It stretched our muscles, quickened our heartbeats, and rested our minds from the serious side of work and academia. We christened ourselves the Unholy Five.

Association with the members of the group began in my student days and lasted until the group dissolved in the late 1990s. Members were

George V. Burger, director of the Max McGraw Wildlife Foundation in Dundee, Illinois; Walter ("W.A.") Isbell, manager and aquaculture specialist in the Department of Wildlife and Fisheries Sciences at Texas A&M University; Edward L. Kozicky, the unit leader at the Iowa Cooperative Wildlife Research Unit and later the director of conservation at Winchester Western, within the Olin Corporation; Robert A. McCabe, professor and head of the Department of Wildlife Ecology at the University of Wisconsin in Madison; and myself.

I can hardly remember the steps taken to develop the alliance. Perhaps I had more to do with it than the others, since I served as a game management consultant on several large cattle ranches in southwest Texas. These ranches provided great hunting, and I was permitted to hunt on them with the group. Our first tent camp was established in the early 1970s on the Apache Ranch on the Rio Grande River north of Laredo on the old Mines Road. The Apache Ranch consisted of about 20,000 acres of typical South Texas brush country. We hunted almost every day of our visits, which usually lasted about a week.

Hunting had its ups and downs. Depending on rainfall and the patterns in which it fell, quail numbers fluctuated between dismally low numbers and unbelievable highs. In some years, we could walk from covey to covey without dogs to help us. Deer in the region were large, many bucks having an eighteen-inch inside spread or more on their huge antlers. We sometimes took a doe or two for camp meat, and W.A. always wanted venison to take home. McCabe and Kozicky did not hunt deer; they were mainly quail hunters. W.A. wanted as many deer as permitted by law, saying he had to take home sufficient venison to last him until mayhaw picking time in the fall.

Our membership never changed. While we invited guests from time to time, they usually didn't stay long. The length of their stay was correlated with the frequency of W.A.'s breakfasts on a stick (discussed later) or the status of the quail population at the time. Aside from traveling Mexicans, we saw few people and no other hunters in our pastures. We may have seemed disparate—two were Texans and three were from the Midwest—but it was as if we had been shelled from the same pod. In the fall we drove to the ranch, each from quite distant places: McCabe from Madison, Wisconsin; Burger from Dundee, Illinois; Kozicky from East Alton, Illinois; Isbell and Teer from College Station, Texas. We chose our camps with water close at hand. Only on rare occasions did we set up a dry camp. Unless it was on the Rio Grande, where we hunted at times, surface water was available only at windmills and stock tanks. Three or four tents were erected for sleeping and storing supplies and food. With all the gear and supplies, the camp site looked as if it could accommodate an army. A fire was always in the center of camp and was kept going almost all day.

Friendship and good will grew from the times we shared. Long days in the field walking miles behind a brace of bird dogs after bobwhite and running after scaled quail were the usual fare. We cleaned our game usually after dark but before supper. Evenings healed any discomfort from sore muscles and poor hunting. Laughing from ribald stories wore away problems. We sometimes bathed in very cold water in horse troughs near windmills because it was the only water available. A Norwegian sauna and roll in the snow could not have been more invigorating than a freezing bath in a horse trough and then racing back to the fire. Life's successes, failures, foibles, and family highs and lows came to light from men mellowed by a mesquite fire and a glass in hand. There was comfort in association; competition showed at times but never confrontation.

Nothing can build stronger bonds in a group of people than shared work and careers, responsibilities, and motivations. Every one of the Unholy Five was known and respected in the national conservation community. Before we stopped hunting together, all had been honored with citations and awards for leadership in and contributions to science and management of wildlife. Kozicky, McCabe, and I had been elected to serve terms as president of the Wildlife Society. McCabe and I had received the Aldo Leopold Medal, the society's most prestigious award, for service to conservation. Our time as the Unholy Five was a diversion and escape from life's serious chapters.

George V. Burger

George Burger was responsible for my getting my doctorate at the University of Wisconsin, where we were students under Bob McCabe. George and I had a five-hour credit class in physics in the early evening hours. Trudging to and from the physics class in deep snow is a memory that remains with me. It was the first time I heard the screeching of snow underfoot.

Not only was George a stout friend; he was stout in math, the basis of all the physical sciences. I was never sure of my math skills. George was my man for math. He almost abandoned me when we were required to wire a Wheatstone bridge (a device for measuring electrical resistance). Our table was a mess of wires, each of which had two ends and no identification markers as to where they were to be attached. George knew. He saved me more than once, and I passed the course and graduated. George hunted with little effort. He sometimes sat by an old trailer that had been used for hauling hay to cattle. Grain had spilled from the trailer and quail came regularly to feed. George usually killed a few quail at the trailer before he joined us and our dogs.

He hunted and pursued butterflies more than quail. A tall man, he was a comical sight racing through the bushes armed with a butterfly net. We laughed, but he was serious. He was an inveterate collector and had one of the most beautiful collections of butterflies in the Midwest. The collection was given to a museum in Illinois at his demise. On several occasions George invited us to hunt pheasants at the McGraw Wildlife Foundation Research Game Farm near Dundee, Illinois, where we were privileged to mop up the pheasants that had been released and hunted by parties from the Chicago area.

I always enjoyed talking with George. He had a keen and wide-ranging intellect. A fan of the Indian nations and interested in the wars that the United States had fought after the American Revolution, he knew all about the Battle of the Little Bighorn and Custer's mistakes and told about them as if he had been there. He also enjoyed western stories. *Lonesome Dove* was a favorite of his and mine, and we often talked about Larry McMurtry's talent in developing characters. One never quite knew when George was being serious because he laughed or chuckled during most of our conservations.

Around the campfire one night, George complained several times about smoke getting into his eyes. W.A. said to him, "George, you're a Ph.D. Get up and move."

Walter A. Isbell

W.A. was the self-appointed cook for our camp. He brought to our camps all manner of iron cooking pots, racks for cooking over an open fire, and vessels in which to heat water. Tin plates, cups, and other culinary gear added another hundred pounds or so to his pick-up load of camp gear. He was an excellent cook during the first days in camp. Hearty breakfasts of bacon, sausage, eggs, coffee, toast, and jams were the order of the day. As the days wore on, the fare changed.

While cooking the evening meal, he sometimes had rum and coke or a margarita in a half-liter plastic Coca-Cola bottle with the top cut off. He was never garrulous or testy after an evening with José Cuervo. He became a philosopher and storyteller. On the third day in our camp, after a night with his favorite rum or tequila, we were served breakfast with a slice of bread on a stick toasted over the fire. Alcohol was actually used in moderation in our camp, but we watched the rum after that One evening, W.A. came to me and said, "Jim, George is after my job."

"What do you mean, W.A.?" I asked. "What job?"

W.A. replied with perfectly serious demeanor, "Camp drunk."

He brought hilarity and laughter to our camps and to other places too. Stories about him in his home town are priceless. He never let an opportunity pass to write to the local newspaper about the news in the area or in the world at large. The people at the paper knew him and always printed his letters to the editor. Some of his best material was directed at the foibles and failures of politicians after they were elected to public office.

W.A. was interested in aquaculture and became the manager of the aquaculture center at Texas A&M. I could always depend on W.A. for practical advice—and honesty—in dealing with problems related to the fish farm, which he could quickly analyze so as to recommend solutions to the most serious of them. He anticipated needs before they developed. He also operated his own business at his farm, a put-and-take hunting preserve for quail, chukar and pheasants.

W.A. and his wife Sue had five children, all educated at Texas A&M University, and all living at home much longer than most children. W.A. said, "We couldn't get them to fledge, so Sue and I just moved off and left them."

Edward L. Kozicky

I arrived at Ames, Iowa, in July 1950 to begin my master's degree, backed up with very little money and clothes not suited for the cold climate. I had a surplus army field jacket with an inner wool lining, blue jeans, boots, and clothes for warmer climates. Fortunately for me, Ed was not in Ames when I arrived; he might have invited me to study waterfowl somewhere else. He was in the hospital in Des Moines with polio, which was in epidemic proportions at the time. Several weeks later he returned to work, and immediately prepared me for work at Forney Lake in Fremont County. He equipped me with a vehicle, introduced me to the study area, and briefed me on expectations and logistics of my project. As a novice waterfowler, I learned to identify ducks quickly.

Ed did not visit me often on my study area. He and Professor George O. Hendrickson came to see me in late fall, and I didn't see Ed again until December when I returned to the campus. It was cold during their visit, and the three of us huddled around the large wood stove stoked with willow firewood. We spent a good part of the evening there. I remember Ed remarking that "it must really be cold in Amarillo." On the next morning and many others, I awoke with ice or frost on my sleeping bag where moisture from my breath had collected.

My quarters were a "duck house" where the Iowa Conservation Department treated lead-poisoned ducks. I chose the duck house over a very large, old frame house that featured rats about the size of muskrats. You can imagine the condition of the duck house after several hundred ducks had been kept in there over time. The exterior walls were made of quarter-inch plywood. It was built to contain ducks, not to exclude cold. Undoubtedly, it was the coldest habitation in southwestern Iowa, and it was to be my home for the next several months. My first weeks there included labors to clean the duck stuff from the floor and "winterize" the house by stacking baled hay around the foundation and lower walls. I spent a good deal of time each day cutting wood, mainly willows around the lake shore, and cooking on a Coleman two-burner gasoline stove. Anyone who has any trouble lighting a contrary gasoline stove should call me. I am an expert, especially when the temperature drops below freezing.

In my work I had good direction from Ed. I respected him as no other. I enjoyed the project and achieved my goal of doing research on waterfowl and marshes. Ed's friendship has meant more to me than I can describe. In many ways and at many times, he has assisted me in my career, and like the other members of the Unholy Five, he served as a mentor.

At our hunting camp, melting aluminum beer cans in a mesquite wood fire delighted Ed. We never quite decided if his delight stemmed from the beer or from watching the cans melt. Illegal immigrants were common on the Apache, and it was a major route for drug traffickers from Mexico. Rattlesnakes were common too. Some of the biggest snakes I had ever seen, up to six feet in length, occurred there. We seldom saw a small rattler; they must have been born big! One evening when we were sitting around the fire, our dogs, tethered a few yards away, began to bark furiously. We thought a raccoon or a coyote was challenging them. When Ed went to investigate, he immediately came back to the fire to get a gun. The snake he had discovered was dispatched with some malice. Ed returned to the fire a little paler than usual.

Robert A. McCabe

Bob McCabe was a man of strong character and will. An assistant to Aldo Leopold at the University of Wisconsin, he was an excellent field man and resolute in his endeavors. He spent much of each summer at the

Delta Waterfowl Research Station in Manitoba working with waterfowl and marsh ecology; he got me the ill-fated internship there in 1954.

After my study site at Delta was flooded, Joan and I went to Madison to see Bob. I expressed my regret that I was leaving and promised to find another project and funds to continue my doctoral program. Bob said he expected me not to return as a student, and he made no promises about further work at the University of Wisconsin. He was pessimistic about my future.

On returning to Texas, I contacted the state game and fish agency and was hired as a deer biologist on the Edwards Plateau. Seeing opportunities for doctoral research on the project, I sent Bob a proposal to study the productivity and management of white-tailed deer in the Central Mineral Region of the plateau. He invited me to meet with him at a North American Wildlife Conference in New Orleans to discuss the proposal. He also invited Starker Leopold, an eminent deer biologist at the University of California at Berkeley, and Eugene A. Walker of the Texas game department to sit in with us and discuss the proposal. It was approved, and Bob and I planned the project so that I spent the next five years in the field conducting research on my dissertation at the same time I was performing the duties assigned me by the game department.

I owe much of whatever success I've had in my work to Bob McCabe. He rescued me when it counted. Like Ed Kozicky, he boosted my career in whatever ways were available. He did not want any recognition for his work with students. Bob refused co-authorship on student papers, stating that the work was theirs and he did not deserve credit. His relationships with his colleagues meant as much as his scientific talents. He had conducted research on waterfowl and wetlands and on members of the grouse and pheasant families in North America. He was also interested in international conservation and had projects in Africa, Ireland, and Canada. Studies of field techniques for conducting research were his forte. He favored long-term projects that kept his students somewhat longer than other professors. Most students spent at least four or five years in the field before writing up their results. However, he typically had conservation organizations employ them so that they and their families could devote this amount of time to their projects. We sometimes grumbled about our status as "indentured servants," but no one complained about the value of the experience or the quality of the research under Bob's direction.

Bob loved to camp and to hunt bobwhite quail. He was a good shot. I could always tell when he was having a bad day. When he was a little off, he would bend over at the waist, stare at the ground for a minute or two, and then straighten up, deliver an expletive, and move on.

During some of the years we hunted, quail numbers were very low. We sometimes walked for several hours and put up only two or three coveys. We always walked with our dogs rather than putting them down and following in a pick-up truck. Bob seemed to never tire. He kept us in the field far longer than we sometimes wanted. Even in his mid-eighties he kept plodding steadily along, hardly ever stopping to rest for more than a few minutes. I knew his stamina was failing in those later years because he would let me assist him over or through barbed-wire fences.

His hearing also began to fail. Once, as we were walking with our dogs, I heard a rattlesnake within easy earshot. I glanced over at Bob and a large rattler was within a couple of yards of him. He did not see the snake. I yelled at him, "Snake, snake!" He raised his shotgun to the ready, thinking I was announcing quail, and yelled back, "Where, where?" He was not a bit embarrassed.

Our host at the Apache Ranch was John Blocker, a regent at Texas A&M University. He rarely hunted with us but often visited our camp. We teased him with the comment that we were proud of him for having this large ranch but rarely hunting himself, reserving it for us poor academics.

Because drug trafficking from Mexico intensified, we moved our camp farther from the border to the 67,000-acre Chaparrosa Ranch near Uvalde. The deciding factor was the murder of a tick inspector working for the U.S. Department of Agriculture. He was killed in his shack on the Apache Ranch in a pasture near our camp. Mexican illegals traversing the ranch often came to our camp to beg for food and water, with which we obliged. We usually left canned food in plain sight for them to take while we were away. We had no trouble with them. The Chaparrosa Ranch was owned by Belton Kleberg ("B.K.") Johnson, a scion of the King Ranch Family. B.K. was a great friend and host. We continued to hunt on the Chaparrosa until the late 1990s when several of us had aged and were close to the end. Soon after, B.K. sold the ranch to a wealthy Mexican silver baron.

As the old saying goes, Bob McCabe broke the mold. There will never be another like him. On bright sunny fall days, I think of Bob, my dogs, and our camps and observe to my wife what a great day it would be for hunting quail on the Apache or Chaparrosa ranches. Thinking back on our camps and hunting brings to mind what Teddy Roosevelt said in the foreword to *African Game Trails:* "There is delight in the hardy life of the open, in long rides, rifle in hand in the thrill of the fight with dangerous game. Apart from this, yet mingled with it, is the strong attraction of the silent places, of the large tropic moons, and the splendor of the new stars; where the wanderer sees the awful glory of sunrise and sunset in the wide waste spaces of the earth, unworn of man, and changed only by the slow change of the ages through time everlasting."

HUNTING AND FAIR CHASE

I am a hunter and have been since about age twelve. I have hunted and killed a number of big game species and game birds in North America, Africa, Canada, and Mexico. Hunting has been a great source of pleasure to me and millions of others. It has been an important facet of my life.

Now, however, hunting is the topic of a great debate. Anti-hunting organizations and animal welfare groups have increased over the years. They have been successful in stopping hunting, sometimes to the detriment of the quarry, the economy, and conservation. The stridency of the debate worries me because I fear the great number of non-hunters, most of whom are neutral to hunting, will overwhelm those who hunt.

As a professional wildlife biologist I feel no contradiction in killing individual animals, although I strive to protect species. Management often dictates removal of some animals for the greater good of the population as a whole. Hunting is much more than merely killing animals; if all the enjoyment of camaraderie and being afield were taken from me and only killing remained, I suspect I would not hunt. And without hunting as a source of funds, conservation would be most difficult.

Sport hunting is threatened in North America. The average age of hunters has increased, and recruitment of young people into sport hunting has lagged in recent years. Together these two factors are producing a decrease in hunter numbers. This is problematic in that hunting and conservation are inextricably linked. Most state conservation agencies are funded largely by hunting and fishing license sales, and federal funding is also tied to license sales. The agencies feel the pinch with the decrease in hunters. Few such agencies receive direct appropriations or taxes to conduct their work. Conservation agencies seek to entice youth into hunting and to provide greater services to those who use wildlife resources, whether the use is consumptive or non-consumptive.

I do not wish to defend hunting, as the matter is settled with me. Most people today are well acquainted with the arguments on both sides of the topic. Moreover, I decided long ago that the joys and societal values of hunting cannot be described adequately to non-hunters. In the attempt, reason and good will often give way to emotion and frustration for both parties. If the death of the prey were not the terminal point in the arguments, debate over blood sports would certainly be less vituperative. Animals die. Humans die. Animal welfare and how animals die are grave questions. No one likes the idea, especially when death occurs without reason. Nonetheless, hunting will continue as recreation and as a weighty issue in conservation.

Yet despite my acceptance of hunting, I confess dismay and anxiety with how hunting of big game species is now conducted. Many conservationists, including hunters, believe hunting has been bastardized by gadgetry, contrivances, hunting techniques, optics, and weapons. Some hunters now wish only to take a trophy to display on the wall; they fail to appreciate the purity and majesty of nature, long an essential element in hunting. Wildness in the sense of not being cultivated, or growing without the care of humans, is a characteristic that hunters value in their prey. In the spirit of fair chase, hunters value animals in natural habitats untouched by human hand.

To produce "trophy" or "quality" bucks, deer are intensively managed in natural habitat or husbanded in confinement in Texas and other states. They are bred, sometimes artificially inseminated with semen from sires selected for the size of their antlers. Some sires are selected and mated with females of bloodlines that have produced desirable progeny in previous breeding experiments. They are fed high-protein feedstuffs, vaccinated and doctored as needed, weighed and measured, and selectively mated—practices and technologies normally associated with agriculture and domestic animals. Some never leave confinement and are sold to deer breeders for brood stock or sometimes shot in their pens for their enormous antlers.

A buck with large antlers and body size can be a very valuable animal. It is not unusual for such deer to bring $10,000 as a source of semen. One such animal was recently sold for $450,000 to a large deer farm. Its semen was collected to be used over several years to produce trophy animals. The industry of deer farming is increasing even though some practices that attend captive breeding are not desired by traditional hunters. Certainly, most hunters oppose hunting confined deer and police themselves by using the tenets of fair chase.

Fair chase is a term given to hunting game without unfair advantage to the hunter. It is a code of conduct hunters impose on themselves to give their quarry a chance of success at eluding pursuers. While hunting as a sport has no referees, there are laws and regulations that govern it, and fair chase provides a framework of tradition and behavior. This idea is not unknown in other sports. Society attempts to match strength for strength in horse racing, for example. Horses are handicapped by adding weight to their burden so as to put each contestant on the same plane. Smaller jockeys are required to carry more weight. Golfers' skills are measured and each is given a handicap to make their scores more competitive. The purpose is to provide more even chances among the contestants. It is the same with hunting.

In settlement times, wildlife was a source of food and hunting carried no stigma. There were no handicaps. Fair chase ideals developed as game grew less plentiful and as hunting shifted from a subsistence activity to a sporting one. But today some hunting techniques and management practices subvert fair chase. Searching habitat from aircraft to find trophy animals, baiting game to the gun, using automatic weapons and dogs, and hunting from off-road vehicles are examples of hunting activities outlawed by most conservation agencies. Such conduct is certainly not endorsed by those who hunt within the rules of fair chase.

Texas is known for its white-tailed deer. It is also known for its system of baiting deer to the gun and for unrelenting efforts to produce trophy deer with inside antler spreads of at least twenty-two inches. Blinds are built to provide easy shots toward a feeder filled with corn or other cereal grain. Feeding near the blind commences prior to hunting season to habituate the deer to the feeder. On ranches with high deer density, it is not uncommon for fifty or more deer to visit the feeder in a day.

Commercialization has been partly responsible for denting the aura of fair chase. Long held traditions are being eroded and replaced by the sentiment "been there, shot one, bought the T-shirt, and am entered in the record book." In some respects, big game record books promote ego and competition for recognition. When large sums are paid for leases or for services of one kind or another, hunters feel compelled to get their limit and get the largest trophy—to get their money's worth.

We manage habitat to produce larger antlers and body size than average, and now we have learned how to manage animals for the trophy characteristics hunters eagerly seek. Aldo Leopold offered cautions long ago about intensive management: he said wildness was directly proportional to the artificiality and intensity of our management practices. Veterinary scientists at Texas A&M University have recently learned how to clone deer. To many wildlife biologists, this is going a step too far.

Jack Ward Thomas, Robert Brown, and I put it this way in the *Bugle,* the magazine of the Rocky Mountain Elk Foundation: "The deer cultured in laboratories and feed lots are not 'superior.' They are simply freaks. The title 'Franken deer' seems more appropriate. Such do not deserve the title of 'trophy,' as they are but ornaments produced to assuage the ego of the buyer or the creator—the wizard behind the curtain produced the aberration. Wherein lay the mystery, tradition, and honor associated with centuries of hunting tradition?"

When I first started hunting as a youth, I felt no unease about it. It did not trouble me. As a matter of fact, the question did not enter my mind as a problem of conscience to wrestle with, then or later. I hunted as a matter of course, without guilt or sorrow; yet I know now that my character as a youth contained little empathy for "dumb animals." After a life in conservation work, I am not so sure of my position.

In my view (not shared by many of my persuasion), fair chase does not ring true as a valid defense of hunting. We cannot arm animals with weapons and skills that humans possess and therefore cannot place animals on a level playing field with hunters. The score of any contest between hunter and prey, if there is such a thing as a contest, will always be hunter 1; game, 0. I believe other arguments—biological and economic, for example—must be made to justify hunting.

I am a professional member of the Boone and Crockett Club, an organization with a founding emphasis on conservation of wildlife, fair chase, and trophy animals for its record book. Founded and led by Theodore Roosevelt, the club was the first major conservation organization in the New World. It was responsible for the beginning of the conservation movement. Many prominent scientist-conservationists are members. Obviously, members of the club have come to terms with hunting, as I have. However, worries linger about how we conduct the sport.

Fair chase is one of the supporting pillars of the Boone and Crockett Club. It is practiced to the extent that membership requires an applicant to have killed at least two big game animals in fair chase. When accepted, the applicant pledges to adhere to rules of the fair chase hunt; most members probably do so, but they number only a fraction of the nation's hunters. Further, the Boone and Crockett Club has voted not to accept into its big game records any game animal killed inside a high-fenced area, no matter how much land lies within the fence. The club has decided that no animal in confinement can be considered free, and fair chase would not apply. This is one measure that I think the wider hunting fraternity sorely needs to embrace, even if many of us still have uneasy reservations about the doctrine of fair chase when animals confront the skills and equipment of a modern hunter

As a university professor, I know that students are vexed by the question of recreational hunting, and their opinions reflect those of the general population more than those of their forebears. Most students entering university education in wildlife and fisheries sciences come from urban environments; they lack the kinship to the land that our parents and grandparents often had. Students are now almost evenly split between the sexes, and many women want to train for careers as wildlife veterinarians, conservation educators, and laboratory scientists or in other roles that do not involve hunting. The decisions we make about hunting are highly personal. My suggestion to students is to review as many perspectives as possible to identify a comfort zone.

CHAPTER FIVE

The Context of Conservation

I HAVE always regarded Isaac Asimov, a world authority on science and medicine, with awe. In more than 470 books, he captivated me and thousands of others like me with his forecasts of events and problems in the conservation and protection of the natural world. For many, his stature in science and his broad intellect gave credibility to his reasoning and predictions.

Asimov put conservation into the context of world affairs; that is, in the context of the political, socio-economic, and scientific future of the human condition. His assessments and judgments of how we are treating the planet were not very appealing or encouraging to the conservation community or to society at large. But like the prognostications of other intellectuals, his appraisals of human intemperance in the natural world and where it is leading us are largely ignored in the affairs of most nations.

One of Asimov's short estimations of the place of conservation in the overall structure and thrust of human endeavor was published in, of all places, an advertisement in *Science*. It was not a lengthy or diffident statement. He placed conservation at the very bottom of societal concerns. Not surprisingly, many indicted him as an alarmist and challenged his ranking as too severe. Asimov said:

> We are living in an age where many scientists are thinking big. There is the supercollider, a new unprecedented powerful particle accelerator which will give us an answer at last to the final details of the structure of the universe, its beginning, and its end.

There is the genome project, which will attempt to pinpoint every last gene in the human cells and learn just exactly how the chemistry of human life (and of inborn diseases) is organized.

There is the space station which will attempt, at last, to allow us to organize the exploitation of near space by human beings.

All these things, and others of the sort, are highly dramatic and will be, at least potentially, highly useful. All are also highly expensive, something of great importance in a shrinking economy. Worse yet, all are, at this moment, highly irrelevant. What is relevant is that we are destroying our planet.

Since there can be nothing on Earth, simply nothing that is more important than saving the planet, our coming priorities must be to reverse these destructive tendencies.

I regret this, for I am emotionally on the side of the big projects, all of them, but necessity is a hard task-master, and necessity is now in the saddle and holds the whip.

Losses in environmental quality and losses of wildlife and its habitat in the last two centuries have exceeded losses that occurred in the long earlier history of humanity. Losses to the natural world are accelerating even today and are directly linked to the growth of human numbers. The context in which conservation is practiced is terribly difficult as society usually deals with problems of the moment and neglects the long-term results that slowly but inexorably develop.

POPULATION, DEGRADATION, AND CONSERVATION BUDGETS

Human numbers are the central cause of the destruction of the natural world. Here are the statistics that have put or will soon put worldwide numbers of humans beyond the amount of resources needed to sustain them.

Demographers tell us that 6.2 billion humans inhabit the earth and that another billion are added about every ten to twelve years. The global birth rate is near 3 percent, and while it is decreasing in some nations, populations continue to increase. Reproductively viable females remain for longer periods in the population. Improved health care has increased human longevity, and death rates are declining.

Why should we worry about human numbers? Poverty is the greatest enemy of conservation. Profligacy, chicanery, corruption, over-exploitation, and waste of resources are the products of poverty. Human numbers are the root cause of poverty and are the specter that looms over all we do.

Conflicts over uses of resources are the inevitable result. Demands for resources increase as population increases. To protect the natural world is an increasing burden in those regions of the world that cannot sustain their numbers. More than 90 percent of births now occur in regions of the world that can least sustain more people.

Within the United States, racial and ethnic populations and their distribution are changing. Soon Anglos will no longer be in the majority. Hispanics are projected to reach an absolute majority by 2020. Asians and African Americans will increase to numbers that will likely change political alliances and elective offices. A U.S. population that once was 80 percent rural has now exceeded 80 percent urban, a change that has occurred largely since World War II. Cultures and values of elected representatives will change with all these demographic shifts.

Meanwhile, the budgets of government agencies are abysmally low. They cannot meet even the minimal demands of society to protect wildlife in wealthy nations, let alone in developing nations. Governments have not made the need for preserving the natural world a high priority. Permits, licenses, and leasing fees for hunting concessions are substantial sources of state revenue in some developing nations, just as license sales are in the United States. However, conservation organizations outside the government are largely required to fund their programs without direct appropriation from national coffers.

Conservation of natural resources, including wildlife and wildlife habitats, may have far greater long-term benefits than aid programs providing short-term fixes. Hunger crises often force foreign aid programs of western nations to address the immediate causes of human tragedy, leaving aside the desperate underlying and ongoing problems of producing food for more people or controlling pandemic diseases. Most conservation efforts are doomed to failure if impacts on nature are not considered in efforts to improve people's living conditions.

The explosion in the number of non-government organizations in recent decades is astounding. Citizen groups have arisen in an attempt to compensate for weaknesses in government environmental activity, and they now have an enormous effect on conservation. They number in the thousands and are important players worldwide. Much of the work of these organizations is provided by volunteers, and their financial support comes from the private sectors of society. Some have budgets and operations rivaling those of whole nations. Representatives of citizens' groups often outnumber government agency personnel at the international meetings where conservation issues are debated and decisions are made.

Right alongside the rise of citizens' groups committed to our common interest in the well-being of wildlife in the nation and the world, controversy has arisen since World War II over ownership of wildlife in the United States On one hand, the law clearly states that wildlife is owned by the people held in trust for us by the State. On the other hand, laws and regulations also place wildlife under control of the owner of private property. Access has become a major barrier to hunting on private land.

With landowners aggressively claiming private property rights came changes in deer management, for example. Hunting began to gain strength as a commercial enterprise by landowners, conflicting with the traditional system of common ownership and widespread public access to deer. Standpoints on both sides of the debate have merit and are often related to regional traditions and kinds of game. For close to a hundred years, waterfowl and small game have not been commercially important. Across most of the nation they are usually harvested on private land without cost to the hunter. But in Texas nearly 97 percent of the land is privately owned, and white-tailed and mule deer are for the most part available under the hunting lease system. Commercially styled sport hunting therefore began in this state and grew as the southeastern states followed the Texas example.

Curiously, the most fervent opposition to commercial hunting and private ownership of game came from the seventeen western states and provinces of the United States and Canada. Their position seemed somewhat out of character with their culture and traditions. Most westerners want independence from government; their traditional argument has been that the private sector can manage the public lands of the West, and the private property, more efficiently and profitably than can the several layers of government. It is interesting that the western states oppose commercialization of wildlife yet favor privatization of its habitat through divestiture of public land to the private sector and development on a private basis.

Hunters in the western states have huge areas on which to hunt and to enjoy the natural world. They do not require access to private lands. Further, access fees charged by most land-use agencies of the U.S. government are modest, and some carry no charge at all. A virtual army of hunters from the lower forty-eight states travels to the Rocky Mountain West each year to hunt deer. Hunting big game in Colorado, Wyoming, and Montana has become a tradition. Local people resent sharing their game with non-residents, and regulations in some states serve to protect the hunting rights of residents and restrict licenses available to non-residents.

Transferring Wildlife to the Private Sector

Western delegations to the U.S. Congress have repeatedly attempted to achieve transfer of western public lands to private or state ownership. The so-called Sagebrush Rebellion was a notable effort to sell much of the public land to the states and to private owners. James Watt, President Reagan's secretary of the interior, was plainly opposed to conservation interests on public lands and desired to increase their use for commercial purposes; namely, grazing, mining, and timber and water extraction. The rebellion was the most concentrated effort in the last two or three decades.

Like previous and subsequent attempts, the Sagebrush Rebellion failed. But attempts to convert public lands to private ownership will surely arise again. During troubled times in the Reagan Administration, conservationists were discouraged and somewhat adrift. It seemed that all sides had grievances against one another. Reagan may have been a great president in other ways, but his agenda was anti-conservation. All Americans are owners of these treasures, and we want the government to protect them.

We can get a sense of what such privatization looks like by reviewing circumstances in Texas, where legislation and management programs have had the effect of redefining ownership of wildlife, transferring it little by little to the private sector. Most of the relevant laws passed by the Texas legislature have been beneficial and have been championed by landowners and hunters alike, although some laws have favored commercial interests and their worth in management has been questioned.

The Texas Parks and Wildlife Department is charged with providing opportunities for people to hunt, fish, and enjoy outdoor experiences—with providing equitable distribution of wildlife. But obviously, the law cannot package wildlife so that every person gets a share. Trespass laws control access to both private and public property. They were intended to prevent poaching and illegal uses of wildlife but have also had the insidious effect of indirectly transferring ownership of wildlife to those who control access to the land.

In the late 1930s and 1940s, a handful of landowners in west-central Texas enclosed their property with net wire fences eight to nine feet high. They sought to confine their deer and exotic big game species so as to manage the animals according to their objectives. Trophy deer carrying antlers with an inside spread of at least twenty to twenty-four inches became the standard of successful management in the state. To improve or enhance their deer through genetic and nutritional techniques, deer were fed high-protein food and were selectively harvested to remove "undesirable" genetic material. High fences excluded deer with unwanted genetic material from outside the confined herds.

Al Brothers and Murphy Ray, two young biologists with the Texas Parks and Wildlife Department, described the system in *Producing Quality Whitetails* (1975). It was quickly adopted by landowners in South Texas and the southeastern United States. In *Quality Whitetails* (1995), edited by university scientists Karl Miller and Larry Marchinton at the University of Georgia, the system was modified somewhat, which further increased its popularity. It was an epiphany of sorts for deer management.

As already noted, in recent times, ranchers have also attempted to improve their gene pools by releasing trophy deer into their herds to serve as sires—the $450,000 animal mentioned was an outstanding buck with a Boone and Crockett Club score of more than 250 points—and now scientists at Texas A&M University's School of Veterinary Medicine have cloned a buck. Not all deer hunters are pleased with these events. At what point in this trajectory is wildness irreparably compromised? Where does fair chase fit into the picture? Does a profitable corporate project qualify as a conservation success story?

And where will it all end? Are we to expect that in time, cloned bucks may sire offspring that will grow antlers as large as those of the Irish elk, seven to ten feet in outside spread? Whatever would Isaac Asimov say? From his advertisement in *Science,* I think he might not be too perturbed even if the offspring turned out to be unicorns. He considered even the largest human projects to be irrelevant distractions from the main business at hand. What is relevant, he said, is that we are destroying our planet.

FURTHER READING

Teer, James G., and N. K. Forrest. Bionomic and Ethical Implications of Commercial Game Harvest Programs. *Transactions, 33rd North American Wildlife and Natural Resources Conference* (1968): 109–18

Teer, James G. Texas Wildlife: Now and for the Future. Pages 9–20 in *Proceedings of a Symposium, Wildlife Resources and Land Use,* ed. John Baccus. Austin: Texas Chapter, Wildlife Society, 1983. 199 pages.

Teer, James G. Commercial Utilization of Wildlife: Has Its Time Come? Pages

73–83 in *Commercialization and Wildlife Management: Dancing with the Devil,* ed. A. W. Hawley. Malabar, Fla.: Krieger Publishing Company, 1993. 124 pages.

Teer, James G. Trends in Ownership of Wildlife Resources: Who Owns Wildlife Anyway? Paper presented at the Second International Wildlife Management Congress, Godollo, Hungary, 1998. 22 pages.

Teer, James G. Texas Wildlife Fourteen Years Later. In *Texas Wildlife Resources and Land Use,* ed. R. C. Telfair II. Austin: University of Texas Press, 1999. 404 pages.

Teer, James G., and Task Force Committee on Conservation. *Taking Care of Texas: A Report from George W. Bush's Task Force on Conservation.* Austin: State of Texas, 2000. 49 pages.

International Conservation

Teer, James G., and Wendell G. Swank. International Implications of Designating Species Endangered or Threatened. *Transactions, 43rd North American Wildlife and Natural Resources Conference* (1978): 33–41.

Teer, James G., United Nations Development Program Consultant. The Joint Evaluation Mission of the Government of India/FAO/UNDP Assistance for the Establishment of the Wildlife Institute of India. Project IND/82/003. 1988. 69 pages.

Teer, James G., and Wendell G. Swank. International Conservation—A Challenge to All. *Transactions, 55th North American Wildlife and Natural Resources Conference* (1990): 434–43.

Teer, James G. Rangeland Habitat: Its Evaluation and Management for Wildlife. Pages 175–94 in *The Development of International Principles and Practices of Wildlife Research and Management: Asian and American Approaches,* ed. S. H. Berwick and V. B. Saharia. Delhi: Oxford University Press, 1994. 481 pages.

CHAPTER SIX

Texas Parks and Wildlife Department

MY FIRST job with the Texas Game, Fish and Oyster Commission (now the Texas Parks and Wildlife Department) was as the assistant manager of the Gus Engeling Wildlife Management Area, a beautiful example of East Texas timberland. Land around Bethel and Tennessee Colony, Texas, some of which came to be a part of the Engeling WMA, was for many years the site of the national field trials for bird dogs. During the years leading up to World War II, quail were numerous in this area, although by the time I arrived they had declined as a result of intensive use of the land for farming and livestock grazing.

After Gus Engeling's murderer had been caught, I was assigned to conduct research and develop a management plan to restore quail numbers on the Engeling WMA. W. C. Glazener, the director of wildlife restoration at the commission, sent me to Canadian and Buna, Texas, for two weeks each to work with A. S. Jackson and Daniel Lay. These two men were the very top experts in quail biology and management in the nation. I was to learn the essentials of quail in two weeks! To work with both of them in the field was indeed a learning experience. Then John M. Carlisle was appointed to take Gus's place as the new manager of the Engeling area, and his gentle counsel and friendship during the two years I worked with him were as nurturing as that of any mentor I had in those formative years.

My tenure with the state agency was interrupted for several years beginning in 1953, when I took a teaching position in the Department of Zoology and Entomology at Mississippi State University, a job I had applied for earlier but did not get because I had not completed my doctorate. When the position came open again, I took it. Unfortunately, the quail project at Engeling folded after I left.

Work in a state wildlife department proved to be a valuable experience for teaching wildlife science and management. My colleagues were the best field men I had known. I am convinced that employment in a conservation agency should be a requirement for employment in academia. Clearly, university professors would profit greatly by having experience in the field before being let loose in the classroom.

Dr. Ross Hutchins, the head of the department at Mississippi State University, advised me when I arrived that I would need my doctorate to remain on the faculty. He asked me to pursue it during summer sessions, which to my mind was not a good plan; after one year at Mississippi, I resigned to work full-time on my degree at the University of Wisconsin in Madison. Two years of coursework on the campus at Madison followed, and then the flooding disaster undid my plans for a waterfowl project at Delta. In May 1955, my wife Joan and I and our two children moved to Llano, so that I could resume working for the Texas Game, Fish and Oyster Commission, but this time I would also be gathering data for my dissertation.

The two purposes of the project buttressed each other. The state needed information on the deer in the Central Mineral Region of the Edwards Plateau, where the herd had density problems, and I would collect data on deer ecology and management to satisfy my dissertation requirements. As already mentioned, Bob McCabe, chair of the Department of Wildlife Ecology at Wisconsin, agreed to serve as my major adviser. The project proposal was also reviewed and accepted by Gene Walker of the Texas Game, Fish and Oyster Commission and by Dr. A. Starker Leopold, a noted big-game scientist and professor at the University of California at Berkeley. We lived and worked in the beautiful area around Llano from 1955 through early 1961 before returning to the University of Wisconsin, where I analyzed the data, wrote the dissertation, and completed the requirements for my doctorate.

THE DEER WARS

My second period of employment by the now Texas Game and Fish Commission was thus a six-year field study of the state's huge population of white-tailed deer. I was assigned to work on the reproductive ecology and population management of deer in the west-central region of Texas, which In the 1940s (and to the present) had the highest deer density in the state. Populations reached a deer to four or five acres on the granite

Over 3,500 reproductive tracts of white-tailed deer were collected from hunters and examined for studies of the productivity of the Llano Basin deer herd.

soils of the Llano uplift in the Central Mineral Basin and on some lime-stone soils of the Edwards Plateau. Mortality of deer to nutritional de-ficiencies and screw worm infestations in the navels of newborn fawns and birth wounds of does contributed to major annual losses. More deer died from natural causes than were taken by hunters, a fact ranchers of the region often challenged. However, mortality to natural causes was not sufficient to control their numbers, and the dense herds resulted in decreases in antler and body sizes. The problem was and still is well known in herbivore ecology, and it was simple: too many deer. Unless their numbers are controlled, deer multiply beyond the ability of their habitat range to support them. The common solution was to reduce their numbers by shooting them.

Because deer were a major source of income through hunting leases, they were a valuable commodity to the ranching community. Landown-ers were reluctant to kill the number required to relieve overuse of range vegetation and reduce die-offs from malnutrition. They were especially opposed to killing antlerless deer.

To solve the problem of too many deer, we set out to convince land-owners and others that antlerless deer (does and fawns) must be killed along with bucks to reduce the herd to a level compatible with food supply. The desired reduction could not be accomplished by taking bucks alone. It was tough for many landowners to accept the idea of killing females and their young. They contended that taking does would soon eliminate breeding stock from which their bucks came.

It was essential that landowners accept this premise or else little could be accomplished. An elaborate set of census transects for population estimates were established to demonstrate the problem and set harvest quotas. Check stations and data-gathering systems were used to obtain the data. We made an annual census of the herd, counted and aged the kill, estimated birth and natural mortality rates, and began a campaign to educate hunters, landowners, and anyone interested in deer management. My colleagues and I spoke about deer management to civic clubs, agricultural meetings, schools, hunting clubs, and just about any audience that would invite us. We wrote news articles and stories for the media. We addressed county commissioners' courts of most counties and held hearings in the county seats each year to go over regulations and harvest rates. Some of these hearings were volatile and ended in fierce debates and exchanges.

By 1962, the program was building on several years of success. Many

Field studies of known-age deer are important in interpretation of age-specific population performance. Deer are fitted with numbered metal ear tags for this purpose. Photo courtesy the Texas Parks and Wildlife Department.

ranchers who did not participate in the antlerless harvest in the early to mid-1950s began asking for permits to reduce deer numbers on their ranches. The taking of antlerless deer greatly increased until the harvest was divided almost evenly between bucks and does. Llano County, the county with the greatest density of deer in the Central Mineral Basin, harvested over fifteen thousand deer in a single season in 1958. The figure was accurate because every deer taken, male and female alike, had to be reported at a check station established for that purpose.

Die-offs of deer became less frequent and not as great as in previous years. Increases in the number of fawns and their survival rates and in body and antler sizes resulted from the antlerless deer harvest programs.

From my experience in deer management, I am convinced that reason will prevail if facts are provided. Ranchers and other land managers may initially receive new ideas and recommendations with suspicion and reluctance. Like farmers deciding to plant new crops or adopt new machinery and tillage practices, most landowners want to see successful demonstrations of new ideas before adopting them. This was clearly true with our efforts to sell an antlerless deer harvest in west-central Texas.

All counties in the Edwards Plateau, Central Mineral Basin, and most other ecological regions in the state with large numbers of white-tailed deer now have either-sex seasons and habitat management programs for enhancing the quality of their herds. The Texas Parks and Wildlife Department sets harvest quotas for landowners and provides management recommendations for improving their deer habitat. Every now and then, one is able to identify events and management programs that truly made a difference in wildlife management. The adoption of either-sex deer seasons in Texas in the mid-1950s was one of them. White-tailed deer are now more efficiently managed, the harvests of high quality deer are much larger than before, and losses to natural mortality have decreased. To convince ranchers to return to the bucks-only law would probably not be possible now.

MARK A. MOSS AND DEER MANAGEMENT: A CASE HISTORY

Mr. Moss answered the telephone with his standard greeting, "Hello, this is Mark A. Moss, Mark as with a pencil, 'A' as in apple, and Moss as on a tree. We sell cattle and horses. What can I do for you?" He used this greeting because the single telephone line to his ranch usually had interference from being strung from tree to tree. It tickled him to see the expressions on his visitors' faces when he greeted them. Wearing knee-high boots, a black high-crowned hat with a four-inch brim, and a red bandana, Moss was the picture of a rancher with years in the outdoors written on his seamed face. He also was a kindly man, a man whom I respected and knew as a friend.

"Mr. Moss, this is Jim Teer, biologist with the Texas Game, Fish, and Oyster Commission," I replied. "I've been on your place several times. We've conducted deer censuses there. You've been one of our chief co-operators in wildlife affairs in the county. We appreciate and thank you for your leadership.

"I'm sure you know that the game department is holding a meeting of landowners at the courthouse in Llano about the upcoming deer season. We've completed our deer surveys in the county and will present our findings for setting the season and bag limits for deer in 1955. For the first time, we will recommend that antlerless deer be legal game in Llano County. We'd like for you to attend. You can be sure that there will be a heated debate. Some will object and some will approve."

I went on to tell him that the recommendation to reduce the deer herd by taking antlerless deer had been received with animosity by ranchers in Mason County, but they eventually went along with it. That was in 1954, the first year that does and fawns were made legal game in the state. A year later we were attempting to start the program in Llano.

"Yes, I'll be there and will present my side of the argument. I'll bring my brother, Luke, with me and my wife, Martha. She'll want to do some shopping. We don't get to town much. What time does it start?"

"The meeting will begin at 7:30 P.M. and will last as long as needed," I said. "I expect we will be finished by 9:30. We need your help, Mr. Moss. The county is split over this issue and feelings are running high."

"What do you want me to do?" Moss asked. "I'm not much at talk-ing to large groups, though most in attendance will be friends. I may get through my talk with that group. Most of them know my position any-way; I have some reservations about taking does."

Members of the Moss family were pioneer settlers of the county. Sev-eral of their menfolk fought in the Texas war of independence from Mex-ico and were rewarded with several sections of land for their services. They had increased their holdings over the years by purchasing addi-tional acres. A good part of southern Llano County was "Moss country." We needed leaders in the community to endorse the plan. Die-offs of the herd from time to time were almost inevitable as food supplies were re-duced from overuse and periodic droughts. Thousands of deer were lost, and the quality of the herd had deteriorated.

Moss was a "horse man." He had selected an area of granite outcrops in Llano County for his ranch. As a horse breeder, he knew the value of the mixed vegetation that the granite soils supported, from which his horses' strength and stamina were built. He knew the range was resilient after drought and overuse. With rain, it was quick to recover. Like most people of the land, he needed some on-the-ground evidence that shooting antlerless deer was a good management practice.

We conducted deer censuses during September and October throughout the region. A crew of biologists and technicians walked twenty to thirty two-mile census lines in each county to obtain data for use in setting season dates, bag limits, and hunting methods. We were in the field Monday through Friday every week. It was a busy time, and much depended on the data we collected.

I was appointed project leader after biologists Gene Walker and Bob Ramsey had successfully laid the groundwork by establishing the first antlerless deer hunt in Mason County. Joan and I lived in Llano while I was doing this work for the game department in the Moss country and several other counties in the Central Mineral Basin; at times our area included Travis and Hayes counties to the east as well as several counties in the Trans-Pecos of West Texas. The Central Mineral Basin was a beautiful landscape with huge granite outcrops and uplifted monoliths scattered throughout the area. No one knew at the time that Enchanted Rock, a granite monolith in Moss country, was to become a popular state park.

This was the best job I ever had in conservation. Although I had rewarding work in several agencies and organizations, nothing measured up to the enjoyment, camaraderie, and sense of accomplishment that field biology gave me.

THE PUBLIC HEARING

Few issues in game management have elicited as much emotion and anger as did the placement of antlerless deer (does) on the legal game list. This was a national issue, and practically all the major deer states— Wisconsin, Michigan, Pennsylvania, and New York—had experienced the rancor of the debate. Now it was our turn in Texas.

The meeting was held in the courtroom of the Llano County courthouse, which was crowded with landowners and others, some of whom were only peripherally interested in wildlife. Most came in their automobiles; some came on horseback. The program was short and lively. I presented a talk about deer management. Several ranchers, including Mark Moss, talked for several minutes. There was no consensus expressed by the speakers. It seemed that everyone had conflicting views, at odds with the game department and with one another. Most people were well behaved and sincere in their comments. Many opposed taking females because deer had become commercially important, and the ranchers did not wish to lose income by limiting the number of fawns produced.

Mark Moss stowed his notes, written in longhand, in his high boots. As he finished with each sheet prompting his talk, he reached into his boot and brought up another. He was eloquent and firm as he came down on the side of antlerless deer hunts. We could see that his influence showed in the demeanor of the other ranchers. However, the decision was not reached that night.

For weeks the issue resonated in and out of coffee shops, churches, schools, auction barns, and any place where people gathered. Some violence erupted, though it took no heavy toll, and some long-standing friendships were strained. On one occasion, two neighboring ranchers met at a deer camp and fought until they were separated. One had been patrolling his fence line to keep his deer safe from doe hunters. The other was a strong supporter of antlerless seasons. One was knocked into the campfire. Fortunately, his burns were not severe. Several months elapsed before the county commissioners finally adopted the recommendation. The first antlerless deer season was held in Llano County in 1955.

After the public meeting, I wrote an article for *Texas Game and Fish* magazine about deer management, the need to reduce herd numbers, and the struggle to gain acceptance for hunting antlerless deer. My article, titled "Of Nature, Deer, and Man," was published in 1956, more than fifty years ago. Even at this distance in time, it captures an important milestone in deer management in Texas. Llano County became known as the "Deer Capital of Texas," and the recreational and commercial value of deer was and remains enormous. Income from hunting rivals and often exceeds income from domestic livestock, and it has helped keep many landowners on the land.

Moss became a strong advocate of the new law. He opened his ranch to "doe hunting," and during the hunting season of 1958, hunters killed more than 850 deer on his 8,700-acre ranch, almost a deer to ten acres. Most were does. I will always be grateful for Moss's help at that crucial turning point for deer management in Texas.

POLITICS AND DEER MANAGEMENT: UNEASY PARTNERS

The Texas Game, Fish and Oyster Commission was governed by a six-person board or commission appointed by the governor. Membership on the commission was (and still is) a highly sought after appointment by citizens interested in hunting and wildlife management. In 1951, the

The white-tailed deer is the most abundant big game animal in North America and consequently the most thoroughly studied. In the Llano Basin of Central Texas, the population averages about one deer to four or five acres. The deer harvest of fifteen thousand animals in Llano County in 1958 was perhaps the largest in a single year in any region of comparable size in the United States.

number of commissioners was increased to nine to provide representation to the state's major ecological regions.

As each commissioner completed his or her six-year term, a frenzy of lobbying began to fill the vacancy. Without financial contributions to the governor's re-election campaign or status as a celebrity or wealth and visible position, a person's chances for an appointment are slender. Many other appointments made by the governor carry more weight, but an appointment to the state game commission is always among the top choices for appointment seekers. Some people have vied for an appointment for several years before giving up. Few appointees have any conservation or management experience but most have name recognition, which gives them political power. Hunting and fishing license revenues fund most of the programs in the agency, and hunting remains a major topic at the commission's meetings, just as it was during our campaign for antlerless deer hunts.

As game biologists, our work had not ended when we had completed our fall deer surveys. We were required to present our findings and recommendations to the commission for the upcoming deer season. These were always scary times for the biologists because some of the commissioners were opposed to killing does, the very source of income-producing bucks. Having considered the recommendations, the game commissioners were required to present their findings to the county commissioners' courts for approval.

After several months of studying the deer herds and writing recommendations, biologists sometimes received little support. "Boss" Peterson, a politician from the Edwards Plateau and longtime member of the game commission, listened politely to my presentation on the need to reduce deer numbers by making antlerless deer legal. Then he declared, "Aw, boys. We don't want to do this and stir up our neighbors and friends." And the recommendation was summarily voted down by the commission. Even after the commission changed its position about antlerless hunts, the commissioners' courts in some counties voted the recommendation down for several years. It was a tough time to be a biologist with the facts. Politics and lack of understanding of the principles of deer management held the resource captive until the buck law was broken and antlerless deer were made legal game for hunters.

FURTHER READING

Teer, James G. *Texas Deer Herd Management: Problems and Principles.* Bulletin 44. Austin: Texas Game and Fish Commission, 1963. 69 pages.

Teer, James G. Lessons from the Llano Basin, Texas. Pages 261–92 in *White-tailed Deer: Ecology and Management,* ed. L. K. Halls. Harrisburg, Pa.: Stackpole Books and Wildlife Management Institute, 1984. 8,780 pages.

CHAPTER SEVEN

The King Ranch

THE KING Ranch is probably the best known cattle ranching empire in the world. Captain King and his partner, Mifflin Kenedy, were steamboat captains who hauled goods up the Rio Grande to supply the Confederacy during the Civil War. The Wild Horse Desert, as part of the region was called, was used by a few ranchers whose land had been granted to them by the king of Spain.

King and Kenedy recognized the potential of the region for livestock and began to piece together vast acreage for cattle and horses. Much of the land was bought from Mexican residents. Some historians allege that many properties were taken forcibly from Mexican owners. Ownership of some of the land held by King Ranch, Inc., is contested in court today.

Famous for the Santa Gertrudis breed of cattle, which was developed on the ranch by Robert J. Kleberg Jr., and for its quarter horses and race-horses, the King Ranch has become an icon in ranching lore and practice. King Ranch is also known for its wildlife and hunting. Members of the King, Kleberg, and Kenedy families have been and are ardent hunters, having managed wildlife on the ranch with dedication and purpose. White-tailed deer, bobwhite quail, and waterfowl are the major species hunted. Wildlife is an important source of income from hunting, and management of the habitat is guided by integrating livestock and wildlife requirements.

At its peak size when it was jointly owned by Captain King and Mifflin Kenedy, the King Ranch contained more than two million acres in South Texas. It stretched southward from Corpus Christi in the north almost to the border with Mexico, a distance of about ninety miles. The

Laguna Madre and the Gulf of Mexico formed its eastern border. Over the years, several members of the King and Kleberg families bought out their shares of the ranch, which accounts for reduction to its present size of about 850,000 acres.

Robert J. Kleberg Jr. sought to expand King Ranch operations into other grasslands of the world. At one time the ranch had an impressive ownership of several million acres of grazing lands in Australia, Venezuela, Morocco, Cuba (confiscated by Castro), Brazil, and several U.S. states. By any measure, King Ranch is a legend in ranching circles. Most Texans take great pride in the ranch and have a sense of surrogate ownership of it. The "beans and rice days" in the early history of the ranch, before oil and gas production began, are now recalled with nostalgic feelings by the present generations of the Kleberg family. Oil and gas production began on King Ranch by the Humble Oil and Refining Company, the progenitor of Exxon.

The ranch has always protected and conservatively used its great wealth of wildlife. Its vast holdings in land and almost pristine habitats are essentially refuges for nature. The ranch controls trespassing and poaching with wardens and fence riders. It employs a small staff of biologists to manage hunting and its lease arrangements. King Ranch has been a source of animals for restocking habitats in other regions of Texas. By the 1930s a great many areas of Texas, especially east of the 100th meridian, had been shot out and their habitats had been degraded. King Ranch supplied white-tailed deer, Rio Grande turkeys, and javelina for Texas Parks and Wildlife Department restocking of these areas.

THE CAESAR KLEBERG GRANT TO TEXAS A&M UNIVERSITY

Until the mid-1960s I had little knowledge of the large mammal fauna outside North America and even less of international conservation affairs. My research had been confined to small mammals, native big game species, and waterfowl. Like most young assistant professors, I worked to make tenure and to establish myself in the department and university. Research was not a top priority in the commodity-oriented College of Agriculture at Texas A&M. Most faculty members in the department were forced to follow soft money and what research they did was conducted on topics for which grants and contracts were available.

While I had not consciously focused my research on a particular species or conservation issue, my dream was to study big game animals in Africa and Asia, although at the time there was little hope for this. I knew most big game species from books and photographs and from the nonnative species that had been released on ranches and game farms in Texas. To work on the great herds of plains animals and their predators and scavengers on the great savanna systems in East Africa was simply out of my reach. Sheer luck seemed the only way it might happen. Luck surfaced in the form of a grant of $1.4 million from the Caesar Kleberg Foundation in Wildlife Conservation (CKFWC), one of the King Ranch family's foundations.

My association with the King Ranch changed my life and work. It introduced me to other parts of the world and increased my responsibilities from handling provincial matters in Texas and the United States to dealing with international conservation issues in Africa and Asia. It gave me opportunities for leadership positions at the university and offices in professional conservation organization.

The change in my career began in 1965 when William H. "Bill" Kiel, resident biologist for the King Ranch, suggested I submit a proposal to CKFWC for funding graduate student research on nonnative species. To increase the number of species for hunting, Caesar Kleberg had released several exotic species of large mammals on King Ranch. Because I had a large part in obtaining the grant from the CKFWC, Dr. R. E. Patterson, dean of the College of Agriculture at Texas A&M, appointed me to direct the program. I had clear instructions from the King Ranch and the university on what we were charged to do in conservation of wildlife in Texas and abroad. I was charged with developing and coordinating research funded by this handsome grant.

The CKFWC granted a total of $2.15 million to Texas A&M over twelve years for the Caesar Kleberg Program in Wildlife Ecology. As many as nine students and faculty members worked in Africa and in the United States on projects administered through the Department of Wildlife and Fisheries Sciences at A&M. Most of the funds were spent in two research areas: nonnative species of wildlife in Texas and the uses of plains game for providing meat to impoverished indigenous people in Africa. We centered the work on the King Ranch and in East Africa. We established partnerships with several conservation agencies with like interests, including the East African Forestry and Research Organization, Wildlife Services, Inc., the National Parks of Tanzania, and several cattle ranches where we worked.

Over and above the direct grants to Texas A&M, funds were made available for special needs, such as the costs of publications and travel. About $250,000 was transferred to the Serengeti Research Institute at Seronera, in the Serengeti National Park, for purchase of four Land Rovers, a Piper Cub fitted with oversized tires, and construction of four dwellings to house visiting scientists, students, and staff.

At the termination of the program, the King Ranch was asked to assist in establishing a chair in the Department of Wildlife and Fisheries Sciences. The ranch gave $750,000 for this purpose, and with matching funds from the university, the Kleberg Chair in Wildlife Ecology and Management was created. The chair has been held by four people since 1969: myself, Milton Weller, Tom Lacher, and Michael Morrison. As director of the program, I met each year with the advisory board of the CKFWC and administrators of Texas A&M to review the research that had been funded by the program. An annual report was compiled and filed with the foundation's board and the university. A publication series, the Caesar Kleberg Research Program in Wildlife Ecology and Management, was created to publish monographs and relevant research materials developed by the program.

Of special importance were the monographs on several nonnative species in Texas, including the chital or axis deer, blackbuck antelope, and nilgai antelope, all Asian animals. Scientific papers and reports on other topics were published in local technical bulletins and in publications of the countries where the work was done.

ROBERT J. KLEBERG JR.

I cannot claim to have been any more than a work acquaintance of Bob Kleberg's, although he sometimes included me in events on King Ranch, and I came to respect him for his talents and achievements. He was a man of great drive, which produced exceptional results in business, finance, agriculture, ranching, and wildlife conservation. On the surface he could appear tyrannical, but on more than one occasion I saw him tear up with emotion. He was a leader, and everyone treated him as such.

He always treated me with deference, if not friendship, for what reason I am not sure. He used the title "Dr." when he addressed me, but his pronunciation of Dr. Teer came out as "Dr. Teeah." He preferred to be called "Mr. Bob," which I found somewhat difficult because of his age and station.

To his family and some of his closest friends he was "Uncle Bob," but this familiar form of address was not welcomed from everyone. John Owen, the director of national parks of Tanzania, once addressed him as Uncle Bob when requesting financial support. Mr. Bob did not say anything, but his facial expression left no doubt about his feelings.

STUDIES OF WHITE-WINGED DOVES

The white-winged dove is enormously abundant in northern Mexico and the Rio Grande Valley of Texas. It is a very popular game species. Thousands nest in huge colonies in both Texas and Mexico. Hundreds of hunters converge in the region during the two- or three-week seasons in Texas. Many hunt in Mexico, where outfitters and guide services are available, the season is longer, and bag limits are more liberal.

The species has spread in recent years in Texas far beyond its traditional range. Many urban areas now have resident populations of whitewings, and the species has increased in agricultural lands in Mexico. The reason: hundreds of thousands of acres of native brush land were cleared and replaced by farms where the primary crops were sorghum and corn.

Although the dove is a popular game bird, little was known about its migratory and wintering habits. As with most doves, it lays two eggs per clutch and may produce up to three or four nests in a season. The extinct passenger pigeon was the only dove in North America that laid just a single egg per clutch, which likely contributed to its demise in the face of market hunting.

White-winged doves migrate each year, leaving Texas in late September or October and returning the following spring. The relationship between the Texas and Mexican populations was not well understood. Were the birds faithful to their natal colonies and where, exactly, did most winter? Were they impacted by hunting in their wintering habitats in Central America? And how did agricultural practice influence their numbers? Until these questions were answered, management was an inexact affair.

More than 70,000 flying-age doves were banded in several colonies in northern Mexico. Traps were often full, with more than twenty in a trap. Returns were less than 1 percent of those banded.

White-winged dove on its nest.

To answer some of these questions, we organized a whitewing banding program in Texas and Mexico with one of my doctoral students, David R. Blankenship, and Bill Kiel of King Ranch. Each spring from 1966 through 1970, we banded birds in several colonies in the northern Mexican states of Tamaulipas and San Luis Potosí. The banding crew consisted of five or six undergraduate students. We set up camp in the colonies being worked and hardly left them for six weeks each year.

About twenty-five welded wire walk-in traps were kept open all day every day for the six weeks. A few more than seventy thousand flying-aged birds were trapped and banded with numbered U.S. Fish and Wildlife Service leg bands. We were constantly moving from trap to trap, banding the birds and releasing them back into their colony. On some days more than twenty doves were caught in each trap. Once emptied, the traps were baited with grain and reset. Many of our banded birds were recovered in Central America. El Salvador was the region seemingly most favored by the wintering birds. Some did not migrate at all and remained in the vicinities of their natal areas.

Banding duties along with keeping our camp, cooking, feeding ourselves, and cooling off occupied our time. The colonies were hot and humid, and I have never seen rattlesnakes as large as they were in those colonies. Fortunately, the snakes were not numerous. Much to the delight of the crew, a river ran near one of our camps. Students were never happier than during their experiences on the banding crews. I have come to know several of them in later years, now with jobs, spouses, children, and the satisfaction doing work they were trained and hoped to do.

Recoveries of bands from our trapped birds were often very low—less than 1 percent of those banded. They were nonetheless sufficient to determine that most of the birds did return to their natal colonies and that there was little mixing of birds fledged in Mexican colonies with those fledged in Texas. This finding alone was worth the effort in banding the birds because regulations could manage the colonies independently of one another.

Kika de la Garza, a U.S. congressman and long-time friend of Mr. Bob, in a meeting of ranchers on the Herlock Ranch in South Texas, told his audience how each addressed the other. Mr. de la Garza said, "Out of deference to his position and power in South Texas, I called him 'Mr. Kleberg.' He called me 'boy.'" Those living in the region understood. Those unfamiliar with the history of the ranch and region did not. Mr. de la Garza's comment brought a roar of laughter from the ranchers.

I visited Mr. Bob several times each year, usually to report on our African studies and operations but sometimes about particular information he wanted. Visits were usually to the Norias Division on the ranch and sometimes to the King Ranch headquarters on the Santa Gertrudis Division. He lived in a small cottage behind the big headquarters house, where he preferred to be when on the ranch.

Mr. Bob was involved in many ranching and wildlife projects. His breadth of interest in national and international conservation affairs was phenomenal. I was always available to him for special projects. On one occasion, a meeting of his friends and colleagues interested in legalizing horse racing in Texas was held at the ranch headquarters on the Santa Gertrudis Division. Some thirty or forty people, many from out of state, attended. He asked me to present information on the wildlife research and conservation projects in Africa funded by the Caesar Kleberg Foundation. Most who attended were also hunters and were interested particularly in nonnative species on the ranch. While wildlife work had little to do with horseracing, one of his great loves, he was clearly proud of the ranch's activities and apparently wanted a program to entertain his guests. I suspect the affair was more entertaining for me than for his guests.

Mr. Bob, a staunch Republican, and leaders of the national Republican Party visited one weekend at Norias. While politics was a major theme of the meeting, time was made for all to hunt deer, turkey, and nilgai antelope. I presented information on our African program and helped guide some of the visitors.

On another occasion Mr. Bob asked me to come to Kingsville to assist Emory, one of his grandchildren, who was writing a paper about wildlife conservation. Emory—then in elementary school and now married with children—along with her sisters Caroline ("Cina") and Helencita, her brother Juan, and their mother, Helen, are active in conservation affairs.

One late fall day, in connection with a meeting to report our activities to the CKFWC, Mr. Bob invited me to hunt quail with him, his lifelong friend Major Armstrong, and ranch biologist Bill Kiel. It was a fantastic experience. Quail were numerous and we shot well. The dogs were exceptionally well trained by the ranch dog trainer, Walter Sandifer. We went from one covey to the next without going after singles. At lunch time we stopped at a great oak mott, where a long table with white tablecloths, napkins, and wine greeted us. We had a sumptuous meal in magnificent surroundings; for me this was a quail hunt to end all quail hunts!

After another meeting with the CKFWC board, Mr. Bob and I hunted nilgai, an exotic species introduced on the Norias Division in the 1920s and 1930s. He armed me with a .358 Holland and Holland rifle, a large caliber I had not shot before. I must have shot at four or five nilgai bulls—all misses. I thought this was surely the end of my work with King Ranch and was considerably relieved when I eventually killed one. The animal was skinned, and Mr. Bob had a local taxidermist tan the skin and make me a full rug that now serves in my office. Field dressed to about 250 pounds, that nilgai supplied my family with meat for almost four months.

Mr. Bob was an urbane person with many interests. Without formal training in genetics, he created the only breed of cattle to be developed in North America in the last seventy-five years, the Santa Gertrudis, derived from crossbreeding of Brahmans and Shorthorns. It is recognized as a thrifty breed and is widely used in the tropics and semiarid lands of the world.

Mr. Bob had a list of ranchers especially in southern Africa who stocked their ranges with Santa Gertrudis cattle. The Kekopy Ranch in the Rift Valley and the Galana Ranch, both in Kenya, and several ranches in Botswana and South Africa bought Santa Gertrudis cattle from King Ranch. Mr. Bob encouraged us to visit these ranchers to establish cooperative studies of game and ranching. They became important study areas for our wildlife research.

He was interested in horses and horse racing, and the King Ranch colors were always seen in major races. King Ranch quarter horses and racehorses were widely known and sold for premium prices. They were always in demand. Two King Ranch racehorses have won the Kentucky Derby: half-brothers Assault (1946) and Middleground (1950); Assault went on to earn the Triple Crown by winning the Preakness Stakes and the Belmont Stakes in the same season he won the Derby.

The members of the Kleberg family were inveterate hunters. Of the four divisions of King Ranch, the 280,000-acre Norias Division was reserved for Mr. Bob. Other members of the family hunted there but only with his permission. Mr. Bob died in 1974, while I was in the Camargue region of southern France to develop a project on the behavior of its famous horses. I received notice of the funeral by cable but could not make travel connections in time to attend. It was a sad day for me and many others who knew this man and his work. An account of my work with

THE CAMARGUE HORSES IN SOUTHERN FRANCE

The horses of the Camargue lowlands, famous as the source of horses for Napoleon's legions of conquest, remain in small numbers in the estuaries and marshes bounded by the two arms of the Rhone River that empty into the Mediterranean in southern France. No longer wild, the horses are now maintained as a matter of history and heritage of the region. Lukus Hoffman, a well-known European conservationist, invited me to visit his biological field station in the Camargue to study the lineage and behavior of the horses so as to retain their bloodlines. My visit to France was one of the most interesting assignments in my career and led to sending several TAMU students to the Camargue for master's and doctoral research.

the King Ranch would not be complete without mention of Mr. Bob's secretary, Mrs. Lee Gillette. A kindly woman with skill and diplomacy in managing his business and personal needs, she was also helpful to me and our projects. She made sure that Mr. Bob received our reports and messages on financial and administrative affairs. He digested them and quickly gave us the decisions we needed.

The King Ranch has had huge successes with wildlife conservation and management projects in Texas and abroad, for which Mr. Bob was largely responsible. At his death, the trustees of the CKFWC and members of the Kleberg family chose to direct their financial support to wildlife in South Texas. While Mr. Bob was truly an internationalist, the decision to feature work in South Texas was probably the correct one because the wildlife industry in that part of Texas is exceeded only by oil and cattle.

NONNATIVE SPECIES IN NORTH AMERICA

Introduction of nonnative species, or exotics, especially big game, is a major issue in conservation and is heatedly debated by wildlife biologists, conservationists, and landowners. Until recent years, federal and state conservation organizations and agencies have steered a wide berth around the matter of exotic animals and have chosen to treat exotics as domestic livestock. Regulations and guidance in releases and hunting are simply not addressed by most state and federal legislation. The rights of landowners to introduce, release, and trade in exotics are protected, and thus exotic animals can be hunted and killed at will in most states.

Early immigrants wanted to introduce animals from their countries of origin to satisfy nostalgic and sentimental ties to their homelands.

Others sought to stock alien species to enhance hunting interests or "improve" on nature. Ranchers today, on the other hand, release exotic big game largely for commercial interests. Hunting of exotics is now a major industry and source of funds for ranchers in Central and South Texas.

Conservation scientists with IUCN have summed up the problems caused by exotics as follows: "Alien species constitute a major threat to ecosystem integrity around the world. Species that have been either intentionally or accidentally introduced outside their natural ranges have caused extinctions and significant alteration of ecosystems. Predation, introduction of diseases, competition for food, water, space and other resources, hybridization, and habitat degradation are among their devastating effects."

According to the Texas Parks and Wildlife Department, more than 120 species were stocked—"tried," in local vernacular—on ranches in 155 of the 254 counties in Texas through the mid-1990s. Of the great many species released, only the nilgai, blackbuck, fallow deer, axis deer, sika deer, and aoudad or Barbary sheep established themselves in free-ranging, unhusbanded stocks in some of the better ranges of native deer and domestic livestock. Nilgai, axis and blackbuck are all from the Indian subcontinent. Many more species are husbanded in captive herds from which some animals have escaped, but practically all these escapes have failed to persist in free-ranging stocks. The interest of private landowners has grown over the years, and Texas is now regarded as the center of the exotics industry in the nation.

Landowners motivated by the commercial value of hunting do not necessarily value the ecological purity of natural systems and the functions that animals play in them. Ranching of domestic livestock has become a difficult if not marginal business, and as landowners seek ways to increase their incomes, exotics have some appeal. Members of the Caesar Kleberg Research Program in Wildlife Ecology at Texas A&M conducted intensive field studies of nilgai and other nonnative species on various ranches in the Edwards Plateau, Rio Grande Plains, and coastal plains and marshes of South Texas in the 1970s and 1980s. These studies raised interest levels among landowners and others. Hunting and trading in exotic animals grew as the number of species and their populations increased to the point of annual auctions of exotic animals being held. These were high-dollar trades and served to distribute and increase several species into Texas rangelands.

As the director of the Caesar Kleberg Program at Texas A&M, I was responsible for directing the research on introduced animals. Although we did not have time or resources to make intensive studies of all major exotics, we obtained valuable information for management of nonnative species. Perhaps as important, we raised cautions and concerns about releases of nonnative large mammals on ranges where native species were themselves valuable as economic and recreational resources.

Because of the enormous interest in and growth of game farms, I conducted a mail survey of the status of exotics in confined herds on farms and ranches in the United States and Canada in 1991. Although the survey was marred by the inability of many respondents to identify the exotic animals on their properties correctly, and many did not estimate numbers, the results did provide a clear picture of the most prevalent species in captive herds. Fallow, sika, and red deer were the most numerous nonnative species held in captive herds on game farms in North America and were also the most numerous free-ranging nonnative species.

With the growth of the game farming industry, exotics have flourished in the last thirty years. Unfortunately, they remain unregulated. They may be transported in interstate commerce, released without prior studies of the suitability of release habitat, raised without regulations to protect native species, sold as livestock, processed as meat for human consumption, and hunted without seasons or laws to protect them from over-exploitation.

THE NILGAI ANTELOPE

For twenty-one years, 1981 to 2002, I conducted field studies of the nilgai antelope on a 6,000-acre ranch that adjoins the Norias Division of King Ranch, where nilgai were first released in the 1920s and 1930s. This study was the longest on any exotic in Texas. It serves as a sort of template for the ecology and management of exotics on game range and large cattle ranches. Data were obtained on the origin of the animals and history of the transplant; numbers; food relationships between nilgai, white-tailed deer, and cattle; movement patterns; major sources of mortality; and cropping as a way to reduce nilgai numbers.

I spent a few weeks in India to compare the habitats of nilgai in India with the ranges where the species had established itself in Texas. The Smithsonian Institution, the United States Peace Corps, and the U.S. Fish and Wildlife Service underwrote the project. Funds were provided from Public Law 480 to satisfy India's debt to the United States incurred in and after World War II. Public Law 480 was an important source of funds for conservation after World War II. It was especially helpful for conservation work in India. The following description is adapted from my "Nonnative Large Mammals in North America," in *Wild Mammals of North America.*

Origin, Numbers and Distribution of Nilgai Antelope in Texas

About forty nilgai antelope were released on the Norias Division of King Ranch in two transplants in the mid-1920s and early 1930s. Records of the releases and the subsequent increase in population are sketchy. King Ranch family members state that Caesar Kleberg, then a U.S. congressman, stocked nilgai for hunting. Stock for the releases was obtained from the Brookfield Zoo and from zoos in Mexico.

The release followed the usual sigmoid curve of increase over many years—starting out slowly, accelerating for a time, and then leveling off. Few nilgai were seen on King Ranch until near the end of World War II, when they reached the accelerated stage of population growth. They became common in brushland and semi-open savanna habitat. According to aerial censuses of the herd conducted by biologists at the Texas Parks and Wildlife Department, 36,000 were counted in South Texas in 1988 and 28,000 in 1994. The difference in numbers is probably due to vagaries in weather conditions during the censuses and changes in visibility of animals in vegetation. Nonetheless, whatever the exact number of nilgai in South Texas, the total is quite large.

Virtually all live in free-ranging herds in habitat that is quite similar to their native ranges in the Indian subcontinent. All derived from the two releases made on King Ranch. Aided by ranchers and game farmers with commercial and recreational hunting interests, the species continues to spread into other regions in Texas. Most releases in other states fail or, at best, result in reaching and maintaining low numbers. Nowhere in the New World are nilgai more numerous than on the King Ranch.

As their numbers increased, many nilgai left the King Ranch and established themselves on about 16,363 square miles of rangeland habitat in Kleberg, Kenedy, and Willacy counties. They are most numerous on several large cattle ranges in the region: the King, Kenedy, El Saus, Yturria, Armstrong, and Robert East ranches. They occur sparingly and in scattered numbers in the northern reaches of their distribution but occur in an average density of about one nilgai to eleven acres in the heart of their range on King Ranch and neighboring ranches.

Nilgai occupy agricultural land in India, where they are protected as bovids, revered by Indians as the "mother animal." Nilgai in Texas are shy and alert. They have flight distances of over a mile when encountered.

Production of wildlife in captive breeding programs has become popular in the past twenty years throughout the world. Nonnative species are released primarily on private land for hunting; for producing antler velvet and horns for medicinal purposes; and to supply skins and other parts for leather and crafts for the tourist trade. The industry is now widespread. Releases of nonnative large mammals have become a problem with some species in particular areas. Competition with native species for food, interbreeding of some closely related species, and the transfer of pathogens and parasites between wild and introduced species are among the difficulties arising. Texas is the center of the game ranching industry in North America, and conservation officials are now researching their legal options with respect to nonnative releases.

A herd of about three thousand fallow deer on four hundred acres near Hondo, Texas. Cereal grains are planted in the paddock and are supplemented with grains and hays brought in.

A small captive herd of red deer in New Zealand. Deer farmers favor red deer because they are tractable, produce large antlers, and respond well to management and husbandry. Sheep dogs can be used with them in large pastures and paddocks. These deer were to have their antlers removed in a few months to collect the velvet.

Technology used in livestock ranching has been developed and used in husbandry and management of captive deer and other species. Artificial insemination, nutritional supplements, and disease control are common practices used in captive deer management. Fallow deer bucks were purchased in Europe for their antler size.

Habitats are quite similar in their native and release ranges. Many genera of plants, including several species of *Acacia, Prosopis, Celtis,* and other species of woody plants occur in both places. These animals seem to reach their greatest abundance at 32 to 35 degrees north latitude in the United States and India, where temperature and rainfall patterns are most similar.

Ecology and Habits of Nilgai

Curiously, few nilgai occur west of U.S. Highway 77 in South Texas on the above-mentioned ranches, although habitat is similar on either side of that road. Traffic on the highway may be a hindrance to them. Regular livestock fences, about 54 inches high, may also deter them. Nilgai can jump fences and readily do so when pressed, but they prefer to negotiate fences by using scuttle holes underneath, which they enlarge with repeated use.

As mentioned, nilgai prefer scrub-brush that has invaded open grasslands and savanna vegetation similar to their habitats in western and central India. Several genera of woody species occur in both their native and their adoptive countries. Ranchers manage their rangeland, especially woody vegetation, to increase forage for their livestock and wildlife. Woody vegetation is removed in either block or strip patterns, making it appear much like nilgai habitat in western India. The animals are well fed, as their body condition and bone marrow attests, and their reproductive rates have easily maintained and increased their numbers during the years of my surveys.

Segregation of sexes occurs at least part of the year. From aircraft, I have counted herds of up to eighty young bulls. Herds of cows and calves are sometimes as large and are most commonly seen in cool seasons of the year. Older bulls, aged by black or grizzled gray pelage, are usually solitary or occur in much smaller numbers. Young are born in almost every month; however, peak births occur in late summer and early fall. Unlike most bovids, nilgai produce twins about half the time.

We attempted to mark a sample of the herd on Norias to determine their social and biological characteristics. Our data came from several months of observations of herd composition, behavior, and movement patterns. Clearly, nilgai are organized in a hierarchical system, as evidenced by herd numbers, sex, and age compositions and by their predilection to defecate repeatedly on the very same site, males and females alike. Feces build on these "toilets" and usually persist for many months and even years. Old mounds measure at least 5 inches deep and 3 to six feet in diameter. Presumably, nilgai mark territories with feces, but I have not seen aggression at these toilets, as occurs in other species with similar habits.

Bulls fight and often kill other bulls. They fight in the customary posture of many antelope—on their knees—each thrusting sharp horns into the neck and shoulders of his opponents. Many are scarred on their forequarters, where their skin forms a protective shield. There, the skin is at least an inch thick, easily twice as thick as on other parts of the body.

Coyotes and low temperatures with cold rain are serious causes of mortality. Coyotes are plentiful and are not controlled. Like deer, female nilgai leave their young while foraging, and young are often smaller in years of poor vegetative cover. Mountain lion do visit the area infrequently, but their numbers and impacts are virtually nil. Hard freezes and snows, on the other hand, although also infrequent, can be a serious blow to nilgai as the animals do not seem to be able to uncover forage under ice and snow or during cold rain. Unlike ungulates in temperate and arctic climates, they do not seem to paw with their feet under the ice to reach forage. In two incidents in January 1973, hundreds of nilgai perished on our study areas on the Norias Division. A tropical species, nilgai succumbed to lack of food when forage was covered by ice and freezing rain for a period of about ten days. To keep out of the rain and wind, they sought shelter on the lee sides of live oak mottes. My companions and I collected seventeen hundred jawbones of dead nilgai, a distasteful chore.

The short answer to the debate about release of nonnative species anywhere is that it is usually problematic in some way. Releases of nonnative large mammals have one or more of the following results: (1) rapid increases in numbers of the exotic beyond the habitat's ability to support them and native species, (2) reduction of food leading to poor pasturage and mortality of both native and nonnative species, (3) introduction of diseases and parasites that may cause harm to native species, (4) interbreeding of closely related taxa (species, subspecies, and occasionally genera), (5) changes in functional ecosystems and compromises and losses in biodiversity, and (6) an accommodation with native species with success in free-ranging populations of nonnative species.

Only one of the six results is positive, and even then only partial success can be expected to endure over time. Although nilgai on the King Ranch do generate hunting income, and people may continue to experiment with different forms of life, few introductions of nonnative forms can be called an unqualified success. Usually, the old adage "two tigers cannot inhabit the same anthill" explains the fierce competition of nonnative species with indigenous forms of life. When the exotics survive, they are often harmful to native species. Yet millions of dollars are spent every year in attempts at "climatizing" nonnative species. We seem to be proving slow to learn this basic lesson.

FURTHER READING

Blankenship, D. R., J. G. Teer, and W. H. Kiel. Movements and Mortality of White-winged Doves Banded in Tamaulipas. *Transactions, 37th North American Wildlife and Natural Resources Conference* (1972): 312–25.

Teer, James G. Exotic Animals: Conservation Implications. Pages 235–46 in *Wildlife Conservation Policy*, ed. V. Geist and I. McTaggart-Cowan. Calgary, Alberta: Deselig Enterprises, 1995. 308 pages.

Teer, James G. Nonnative Large Mammals in North America. Pages 1180–90 in *Wild Mammals of North America*, ed. George A. Feldhamer, Bruce C. Thompson, and Joseph A. Chapman. Baltimore, Md.: Johns Hopkins University Press, 2003.

CHAPTER EIGHT

Africa

STUDIES OF the enormous herds of plains game in East Africa were among the major research programs mandated by the Caesar Kleberg grant to Texas A&M University. It provided the greatest opportunity of my career to work in international conservation, and it also led to other research and education projects in Africa, India, and elsewhere.

A major thrust of our African research was the study of cropping or harvesting of several species of plains game to feed hungry people. In retrospect, I am sure that circumstances converged in the mind of Robert J. Kleberg Jr. to cause him to recommend a cropping program. He had made several visits to Africa to hunt and to promote the Santa Gertrudis breed of cattle. He had also been approached by President Lyndon B. Johnson to participate in the president's Food for Peace program as part of the War on Poverty, which was a major policy initiative in his administration. Mr. Bob accepted the assignment and was made chair of the Food for Peace program. Because he had recently seen the unbelievable biomass of migration of plains game on the East African savannas, he wanted to place game animals in the program as a source of protein for desperately poor people in the region.

In 1968, he went on a fourteen-day hunting safari with two professional hunters, Ian Parker and Tony Archer, who also operated a cropping business called Wildlife Services, Inc. He was mainly interested in surveying game and livestock on savanna grasslands and bush landscapes not unlike those on King Ranch in Texas, and he was enthused about the possibilities of cropping these herds.

Africa is known for its variety of species and abundance of large
mammals, many of which are the objects of sport hunting, tourism,
and commercial gain for conservation purposes. Cape buffalo (pictured)
form herds of several hundred, and more than two million blue
wildebeest occur in the great savanna systems of East Africa.

CROPPING PLAINS GAME

The African research program occupied a good part of my professional
life for twelve years. As project leader, I was required to make one or
two trips a year to Africa. My major duties were to tend to administrative matters and to initiate and coordinate research projects. I conducted
little research on my own but often participated in field work with our
men during my visits.

Lytle H. Blankenship, Chris Field, and Ronald O. Skoog, all experienced biologists at the midpoints of their careers and with doctoral degrees in wildlife science, were employed to work with Wildlife Services,
the headquarters of which were in Nairobi, Kenya. They were to obtain
data and assist Wildlife Services in evaluating the cropping programs and
the relative values of various species of plains game for providing meat.

Cropping for meat and other products had been attempted in various nations of Africa in the 1960s and 1970s. With few exceptions, all
efforts had failed because of limited commercial success. Yet efforts to

reduce a number of "problem" animals in parks and reserves, such as hippos and elephants, had resulted in reasonable success. These efforts were often ongoing, because as animals were removed, others were born or migrated in.

During his safari to Africa in 1968, Mr. Bob kept a daily record. He wrote: "The over-all purpose of the trip and thought behind it was to study game as perhaps a neglected form of agriculture and also to make comparisons of game and domestic livestock as a means of getting the highest meat and protein production in East African areas and with the thought that some of the ideas obtained from the trip could be applied in other parts of the world; especially Texas and Mexico." Mr. Bob and his party killed several species of big game on their safari, but he recorded little about the hunt itself, explaining that he was not attempting "to record fully the details of our safari as it relates to hunting but only to record that part of it that relates to the objectives set out in the heading of this memorandum."

He visited leaders in the private sector and governments of Kenya and Tanzania. Among them were the Kenyan minister of agriculture, named McKenzie, and tourist lodge operator Jack Block, also a director of Ker,

Impala are likewise widespread and are among the species making large mammals the primary attraction for tourists. Nowhere in the world can one see so many species in such abundance as in Africa.

Portrait of a Masai boy not yet elected to manhood in East Africa.

Downey and Selby Safaris, the premier hunting safari organization in East Africa.

Mr. Bob also contacted several conservationists and was hosted by John Owen, director of national parks of Tanzania, and Hugh Lamprey, director of the Serengeti Research Institute. Owen and Lamprey gave an impressive review of plans for the institute and requested funding for it from the CKFWC. Owen was a former British civil servant in North Africa before the winds of change blew through the continent and altered its political structure forever. He was superbly eloquent in his description of the unique Serengeti ecosystem.

At one point during his visit to the Serengeti, Mr. Bob stood on a large koppie with John Owen and several members of his party. Thousands of blue wildebeest, zebra, and Thompson's gazelles were migrating through a sea of red oats reaching as far as the eye could see. The scene was truly one of the great wildlife spectacles of the world. I never learned whether it was true that he was so impressed with the scene as to ask Owen, in jest, if any of it could be bought. He was, after all, a consummate rancher, and King Ranch was one of the largest ranches in the world.

While his emphasis was on managing wildlife to change the human condition, Mr. Bob was also interested in wildlife for its own sake and for the recreation it affords. The great array of herbivores with their

I had opportunities to meet indigenous people in their tribal areas,
including Masai young men, known as **moran** *(warriors). Many took*
bush meat with primitive weapons—snares, traps, bows and arrows—
and sometimes with old shotguns. Community conservation projects,
in which native people shared in wildlife resources, committed them
to protecting wildlife from illegal capture and uses. Such projects are
having an effect in wildlife conservation in Africa and Asia.

Masai woman with a child in East Africa.

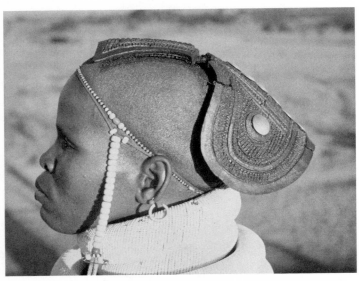

Ndebele woman with a beaded necklace and her hair done up in mud in what was then called the northern Transvaal, Republic of South Africa.

attendant predators, scavengers, decomposers, and other life forms was overwhelming to anyone seeing it for the first time. I believe Owen's talk had a tremendous impact on Mr. Bob. It was probably the defining moment in his decision to support the research and monitoring programs being conducted at the Serengeti Research Institute.

Kleberg was interested in cropping, and so was I, although Owen, Lamprey, and other scientists at the institute did not offer much encouragement for the practice. They were often criticized for protecting such a large resource in the vast savanna systems that might be used to feed desperate people living on the edge of starvation, but most of them nevertheless opposed cropping. Both British citizens, Lamprey and Owen believed that wildlife and the natural world in general should not be used for so ignoble a purpose—that all life warranted conservation in its own right.

The position of park personnel against cropping wildlife in the Serengeti National Park was based on fear of disrupting a rare, functional ecosystem. Taken far enough, removal of essential elements could destroy it. Recall Paul Erlich's explanation of the results of removing elements of an ecosystem. Picture an aircraft, he said. Compare it to an ecosystem. Over the years, remove a bolt or rivet or some other piece of the aircraft. It may continue flying despite the loss here and there of the members that hold it together. But finally, too many are lost, too few remain, and the plane crashes. I agree with the Serengeti officials' decision not to crop animals in the park.

I am torn, however, by the results of their seemingly callous position. In the 1960s, the Food and Agriculture Organization (FAO) of the United Nations conducted a pilot cropping project in the Serengeti ecosystem. The project provided meat to people living on the borders of the park, who habitually poached for food. Meat was dispensed locally for a small price, which partially alleviated poaching troubles. But after limping along for several months, the project was abandoned for lack of political support by the conservationists.

The Serengeti is one of the last large functional grassland ecosystems in the world with animals in major niches that make it so. It was my good fortune to witness the stand on both sides of the question, with positions doggedly held by national parks personnel and humanitarian and utilitarian conservationists. Successful processes for taking large numbers of plains game in wild country were demonstrated by the Caesar Kleberg program in Africa and Wildlife Services, but the effort was out of tune with the times. Cropping of game animals for meat occurs on private lands and for profit but is not acceptable to society when conducted on public property, either in Africa or in North America.

Elephants in ranges where they are exceptionally plentiful can be a serious problem to themselves and other wildlife. Ironically, despite the fact that in some places elephants are endangered and at risk of extinction, in other parts of Africa they are too numerous. They have the capacity to destroy their own habitat, which of course compromises other species as well. The difficulties are often exacerbated by human pressures and interventions in traditional elephant habitats. Elephants are forced to take refuge in parks and reserves, with the long-term effect of damage to habitats on which they and their co-inhabitants depend. Both Asian and African elephants are listed as species of concern by most countries and international conservation organizations.

Crowding in reserves can culminate in starvation and death for thousands of elephants, as happened when more than 3,500 elephants starved in Tsavo National Park in Kenya in the 1970s, for example. Reserves in South Africa and Zimbabwe have seen habitat problems arising when there are too many elephants. But elephants are revered and protected by most cultures and national governments, and world opinion likewise favors protecting them. As a result, even when facing elephant-induced habitat damage, government conservation agencies have generally been prevented from using the one solution that is cost-effective and appropriate—reduction by shooting. In places even low-impact, high-revenue trophy hunting has been limited, with concomitant loss of state income from license and hunting concession fees. In some developing nations, such losses have been devastating to conservation projects formerly funded by the hunting industry.

Other systems of reduction have failed. Attempts at capture and relocation of elephants have not proven a viable solution because of the cost and·the difficulty of finding suitable ranges where they can be released. Chemo-sterility is being tested and shows limited success in some animals. But drugs are costly and often ineffective in targeting viable females in the populations.

A permit was issued to Wildlife Services in the mid-1970s to reduce herd numbers by removing two hundred elephants in the overcrowded habitats in the Mkomazi area of Tanzania, where elephants were damaging the vegetation and using up scarce water. The herds destroyed baobab trees to get at their water content and pushed over other large trees to eat the foliage and bark. I had opportunity to view this project and describe it here.

Wildlife Services set up camp and proceeded to kill their quota. All ages and both sexes were killed. Because ivory and certain parts of the skin—the ears, for example—were valuable products, the margin for profit was somewhat better than that for meat alone. This could not happen today because ivory can no longer be sold legally; elephants are on the endangered species lists of most nations, and international treaties and the court of public opinion aim to shut down the ivory trade.

The social structure of elephants is defined by a small group led by a single matriarch, usually an older female. Several groups may inhabit the same area, but the exchange of members between groups is rare. Members are usually close relatives and may number up to fifteen to twenty females and their young. Young males may be members; older males live solitary lives and rarely interact with the group except during breeding.

Commercial businesses engaged in cropping of elephants strive to take entire groups at one time. Wildlife Services rarely left survivors, which would tend to disrupt other groups and might become dangerous to local people. The slaughter was conducted to ensure safety to the hunters and with efficiency in taking entire small herds in just a few minutes. Following is an account of one such operation.

In the early daylight hours, personnel in a light aircraft searched for a group of elephants suitable for cropping. Upon their finding a suitable band, trucks carrying skinners and butchers were sent to the area. Two shooters then stealthily approached the herd, in this case Tony Archer and Ian Parker. We could only see the backs of twelve animals, young and old, feeding in heavy bush. A young male, almost the size of the females, was attached to the herd but was some distance from it. The elephants were unaware of our presence. To bring them to the gun, the shooters cupped their hands like megaphones and blew loudly. The matriarch immediately came to investigate. When the shooters identified her, they took her down with a well-placed shot to her head. The herd then came and attempted to lift her, and they were shot too. The operation was over within ten minutes with no survivors.

Then the heavy work began. Carcasses were spread over an acre or two. The tusks were chopped out with an ax, and the elephants were skinned. The skin is more than an inch thick in some areas, and the weight is too great for it to be removed all an one piece. White chalk was used to mark the slabs of skin to be cut. Skinners cut along the lines to manage the removal.

Each animal was eviscerated and butchered, and the meat was loaded into the trucks of villagers who came to collect it. Usually meat was either given to villagers or sold to them for less than one cent per pound. The skin was flensed with draw-knives and then salted to preserve it for shipment, usually to Europe or South Africa, where it would be processed into leather.

Until the practice was stopped in 1995, the Kruger National Park in South Africa conducted an annual reduction kill. Thousands of elephants were removed from the park over the years to reduce damage to the habitat. Kruger Park had the most efficient cropping and processing operation of any I saw. Elephants were counted from aircraft and quotas were established for age and sex. From the aircraft they were shot with immobilizing drugs that immediately put them down. A ground crew then killed the animals with rifles and gutted them. To prevent disturbance to other wildlife and to tourist operations, the elephants were quickly winched onto flat-bed trucks and transported to an abattoir, where they were skinned and butchered. The facilities were comparable to what one would see in a slaughter house in North America or Europe. The meat was frozen or canned to be dispensed to park employees or sold to visiting tourists.

Few people have witnessed such operations, but culling nevertheless draws intense opposition. Kruger stopped culling elephants because of national and international pressure against it. After a considerable population increase, the practice was resumed in 2008. Wildlife management is not always pretty. Cropping of wildlife is a grim practice, which may be justified in some circumstances but which also seems to defeat the very purpose of conservation and leaves every observer with deep sadness. Most conservationists understand the problems that reappear after closure of elephant cropping. As a keystone species, elephants have the ability to devastate habitats of all species in their range. To wait until the animals have reached destructive levels, when the alternative to cropping is a death sentence from starvation and disease, is also a sad spectacle. In my judgment, controlled sport hunting should be allowed to prevent the need for cropping. No stigma should be attached to recreational hunting when it is practiced to keep herbivores in check.

HUNTING IN AFRICA

During sojourns to distant places in the world, I have had many opportunities to photograph wildlife and habitats, usually as part of my duties while I was afield conducting research or teaching. My opportunities to hunt the game species of far places were much less frequent. The two occasions that stand out were both safaris in Botswana, one made possible by a friend at Texas A&M and the other contrived by two of my students enrolled in an honors course at the University of Pretoria in South Africa.

Okavango Swamp Safari

My friend John Blocker, a regent at Texas A&M University and vice president of Dresser Industries, introduced me to hunting on corporate leases in Texas and to safari hunting in Africa. As one of John's advisors on wildlife management issues, I conducted censuses and set harvest quotas for white-tailed deer on several thousand acres of land that Dresser Industries leased for hunting. It was a typical South Texas corporate hunting lease, operated from the beginning of dove season in September until the close of quail season six months later. Dove, quail, turkey, waterfowl, deer, and javelina were abundant and carefully managed for sustained yields. Dresser provided first-class hunting and accommodations for the top executives and management staff of their clients.

Hunting was part of business with Dresser, as for many corporations. As described earlier, John maintained that he could sell more oil field supplies and services with hunting than with any golf course membership or family vacation package to Hawaii. It was a splendid arrangement for Dresser. Good will for the company and sales were the result.

Dresser maintained a comfortable lodge and other amenities that were highly anticipated after a day in the field. A professional chef and kitchen staff prepared the food, and it was excellent. Hunters were carefully screened for safety in firearm use, and their guns were sighted in before they went to their hunting areas. Alcohol was available but carefully dispensed. People's conduct was influenced by the knowledge that untoward behavior would result in not being invited back.

James Ross Mickler managed the Dresser hunting leases. His sons, Jodie and James, were yell leaders at Texas A&M. James Ross was a former football player and a rodeo cowboy widely sought as an announcer at rodeos. He was a large man whose knowledge and polite demeanor matched his size. The ambiance he created at the hunting camp, along with the expert staff, contributed to a pleasant experience that even the most jaded and half-spent CEO could appreciate. James Ross had only two unworthy traits. First, he could awaken the dead with his snoring. I once shared a motel room with him but left the room and rented another around three o'clock in the morning. Second, his use of Spanish would have confused even the most educated linguist and was always good for a laugh from the Latinos to whom he customarily laid out the day's work.

After I had been a consultant on Dresser's leases for about three years, John called me one evening and said: "Jim, I am due to visit Africa in late September to see about Dresser's oil interests in southern and East Africa. I want to combine my business with a few days of hunting in the Okavango Swamp in Botswana, one of the great game ranges remaining in southern Africa. I want you to accompany me and my sons." He said they planned to take a fourteen-day safari, collecting various species of plains game and also trying for leopard, lion, and perhaps elephant.

"You know African game and it would be nice to have someone with that knowledge go with us. Anyway, knowledgeable or not, I want you with us. What do you say?" John asked.

I was floored by this invitation but realized at once that I could not go. The cost would be too much for me. An African tent safari for two weeks or so usually ran from $15,000 to $25,000 per person (now up to $50,000), depending on the species to be hunted and the number of hunters in the party. Reluctantly I declined, telling John that although nothing could please me more than to accompany him, he did not need me. The professional hunters would have much more experience.

He replied, "Yes. You are going and you are to take every species we take. Do not think about the cost. My company will pick up a good part of the tab. I will pay all your safari expenses—license fees, and airfare to and from Africa, and incidental expenses. Your experience with environmental and conservation laws in southern Africa will be helpful. So get ready. We leave in about a month." The party consisted of the two of us plus John's son, John Jr., and his stepson, Billy Welder. To accompany these men and hunt in the Okavango was a great experience, beyond anything I could have imagined.

The flights to Africa with a stopover in London totaled twenty-two hours, made comfortable by flying first class. We spent a night in Johannesburg then flew in a light aircraft to Maun, a small town in northern Botswana that serves as the jumping-off point for the Okavango Delta. From Maun, we flew to Machaba, one of our outfitter's hunting camps, from which we hunted for the next ten days. It was a pleasant place with numerous water birds and other wildlife in a palm forest. We moved our camp from time to time to explore for game and simply to see the region. Pom Pom and Savuti camps were equally interesting and beautiful.

The Okavango Delta is the enormous terminal wetland produced by the Okavango River, which empties into a great seasonal swamp in the midst of the Kalahari Desert. It is a unique ecosystem that attracts a wealth of wildlife. It is now threatened by mining and agricultural interests, which require water for their operations.

John had booked us with Safari South; a company that had branched off from the well-known East African company Ker, Downey, and Selby. The professional hunters of Safari South were among the very best in Africa. Each of our party was assigned a professional, mine being Lionel Palmer, a veteran hunter with more than forty years' experience in the bush. We hunted independently of one another. Our professional hunters were expert in putting us on game, and we took several outstanding trophy heads. The party was a congenial and interesting group. The professional hunters made camp life interesting by telling hunting stories. They were knowledgeable in natural history and conservation issues in their region, and they were careful in selecting animals for us to take. Although two of our party hunted for four days for lion and leopard, none killed any of the large carnivores. We each took a kudu, buffalo, zebra, tsessebe, warthog, and lechwe. The skulls were cleaned and the capes were salted and prepared for shipment to taxidermists in Houston.

African safari hunting was unlike anything I had experienced. We spent many hours in Land Rovers and Toyota Land Cruisers searching for trophy animals. Large horns were the goal of our hunts. Several species were plentiful, and we did not have to wait long to find herds to inspect for animals of suitable size. Finding game was not difficult, but selecting trophy heads from the herds required patience and diligence. Hunting for a good kudu, for example, required an all-day drive or several days of driving over sand roads and through heavy bush, binoculars at hand, looking for a bull of trophy quality.

Fair chase is observed by most professional hunters. They require their clients to leave the vehicle and complete the stalk on foot, which can be dangerous if the prey is one of the "big five"—lion, leopard, buffalo, elephant, or rhino. It can be especially dangerous if the animal is wounded and must be trailed, found, and killed. Professional hunters' first duty is to protect their clients at their own risk.

One of my most frightening experiences occurred while hunting buffalo. I was riding in the bed of our Land Cruiser in thick bush as we searched for a herd of five buffalo we had seen earlier in the vicinity, one a good bull with a large boss. We stopped to scan the terrain. I stood in the bed of the vehicle alongside an acacia tree, my head almost touching the tree. When I turned to view another area, I suddenly realized my face was about a foot from a green mamba with its head sticking out of a hollow in the tree. You can be sure I did not say "excuse me" as I left the vehicle in a hurry to put some distance between me and that highly poisonous snake.

Every evening we gathered for sundowners and dinner. There we recounted the events of the day and made plans for the morrow. We slept in tents, ate at tables covered with white tablecloths, and had wine and great food. Our meals were made from our kills. Much of the meat was given to local people. Our campfire talk was filled with exaggerations (not lies) to suit the mood created by our wine. It was every man's nirvana. Two of us refused to go home. I cabled my department head at Texas A&M as follows: "Send severance pay immediately. Valhalla rediscovered!" He did not respond. And in my mind, I remain in Africa still.

Kalahari Desert Safari

In 1969, I was invited to teach an honors course in conservation and wildlife management at the University of Pretoria in the Republic of South Africa. I applied for leave from Texas A&M, and was given a nine-month sabbatical. I taught from February through August 1969. As the course was field-oriented, I had the opportunity to take my class to many of the parks and natural areas in southern Africa. It was an extremely interesting assignment. Time spent at the University of Pretoria paved the way for other African adventures in subsequent years.

At a break between semesters, two Afrikaner students in my honors course, Wally Wise and A. ("Lampies") van Lambrechts, organized a safari to collect small mammals and to hunt big game in the Okwa Valley in the Kalahari Desert in Botswana. We traveled to Ghanzi on the back of a cattle truck, a twenty-four-hour ride over rough terrain, sand roads, and no roads at all. We reached Wally's family's trading post and organized a ten-day safari with only minimal equipment and supplies.

The Wise family operated a trading post in the desert village of Ghanzi, where local people could purchase staples and order supplies from South Africa. On arriving at the post, I was surprised to see dozens of coffins stacked on the porch of the store. It turned out that in addition to being a registered nurse, Mrs. Wise was an undertaker. In this remote region she tended people's health for many years, and she also tended the dead. For her service, Great Britain awarded her the Order of the British Empire. She showed me the framed citation hanging in the feed storage room of the store. She was proud of the honor, but not so much as to display it to all who came into the store. Hers was a life of service and care.

Wally, Lampies, and I set off into the uncharted desert early in the morning of our second day after arrival at the post. We had provisioned ourselves for ten days out. A fifty-five-gallon drum of potable water and another of petrol were essential items loaded onto our old Chevrolet pickup truck. Tinned foods were also mainstays, though we planned to eat the animals we killed.

We set out with some trepidation, not entirely sure that Wally was as familiar with the region as he claimed. We slept on pallets on the ground under bushes with not enough blankets to cover us, ate what we killed, cooked over open fires, were lost from time to time, and nursed our old pickup's breakdowns, from which I sometimes thought it could not recover. We awoke each morning after a night of listening to the sounds of the desert—lions, hyenas, and birds I could not identify. Hunting was good. We took blue wildebeest, gemsbok, and springbok. We met several Bushmen at a borehole (well) and gave them most of our meat, which pleased them very much. Although our Kalahari safari was not nearly as elaborate nor our hunting as productive as what I had experienced with John Blocker's, yet it was simply great. We enjoyed a glorious freedom seldom experienced since.

CHAPTER NINE

The Great Cats

IT WAS my privilege to be contracted for international status surveys of two of the world's great cats: the leopard in the 1970s and the jaguar in the 1980s. Dr. Wendell G. Swank and I conducted the surveys jointly, and both projects were funded by the U.S. Fish and Wildlife Service, National Fish and Wildlife Foundation, Conservation Force, and Safari Club International. In 1973 the U.S. Fish and Wildlife Service designated all spotted cats as Endangered under the U.S. Endangered Species Act, meaning that skins and hunting trophies could not legally be imported. In 1976 the dozens of countries participating in the Convention on International Trade in Endangered Species of Flora and Fauna (CITES) placed spotted cats on Appendix I of the CITES treaty, meaning that trade in their fur was prohibited under international law.

Hunters and the fur industry mounted a challenge on the basis that in most of sub-Saharan Africa, leopards were not in fact endangered, and that the USFWS had failed to gather sufficient data to support an Endangered listing. Our purpose and charge were to obtain a much fuller picture of the true status of the cats.

Our results provided timely information on the state of conservation in developing countries and on the demands made of wildlife by the world. The scope of both surveys was too wide for field work, financially and practically. Instead, we conducted interviews with biologists and administrators of conservation organizations, along with searches of the scientific literature. Information gained was as comprehensive as could be achieved at the time.

The issue of hunting charismatic species of wildlife is vehemently debated in many societies, most of which do not favor hunting African lions, leopards, cheetahs, and other cats in the world. And yet many nations provide little or no protection for the cats that occur in their jurisdictions. The bobcat, mountain lion, and lynx are not protected in the United States, for example. Some are classified as game animals or furbearers, with hunting and trapping regulations governing their harvest, apart from some regional exceptions—the Florida panther is classified as Endangered; a public referendum closed cougar hunting in California; and in Texas, mountain lions lack the protection of game animal status. In Africa and Latin America several other cat species are on game lists and are legally hunted.

Hunters and indigenous peoples have historically killed the great cats of the world as symbols of mystery, stealth, and power. They are highly prized as hunting trophies and for the machismo and beauty they represent. Skins of spotted cats have been a focus of trade for making fur coats, purses, stoles, gloves, and other fashionable wear.

Further, because they prey on animals valuable to humans, cats in many parts of the world are killed opportunistically whenever they are encountered. On ranches running smaller livestock—sheep, goats, calves, and game—cats are trapped, poisoned, and shot. Some species have been extirpated from large areas where the economy is based on livestock. Frequently, cats are also blamed for the loss of big game such as deer and are persecuted. Western states have conducted state-supported predator control programs to protect game animals and livestock. In many places, smaller and some larger species of cats are simply labeled as vermin, meaning that they have no protection under the law. Because cats have large home ranges and roam over wide areas, parks and reserves are often too small to protect viable populations.

Under this kind of constant duress, it is truly remarkable that some species of cats have managed to maintain their numbers. The lion, leopard, and cheetah in Africa, the tiger in Asia, and the jaguar in Central and South America are species of intense conservation interest. In recent years they have been given increased protection and managed with some success by international conservation agencies and home states. However, poaching remains a serious problem where Oriental medicines are popular and cats are killed for the alleged medicinal value of body parts. Some New World cats, like the ocelot, jaguarundi, jaguar, and margay, have been extirpated in North America but remain present in Central and South America.

The skin trade for the fashion industry was the major cause of losses of spotted cats in both Latin America and Africa. Spotted cat skins brought high prices to people who lived on the edge and depended on bush species for their livelihoods. Before the jaguar was placed on Appendix I of CITES, local poachers were enlisted by organized poaching rings to supply skins for the trade. Skins were collected in return for guns, ammunition, food, and field gear. The skins were shipped to Europe, mainly Germany, and to several Asian countries, where they were tanned and made into clothing.

When the first meeting of the parties of CITES was held, the conservation community was quick to recognize the potential for protection it afforded spotted cats. Without much supporting data, all spotted cats were placed on Appendix I, making all uses and trade illegal. The illegal exploitation of spotted cats and smuggling of skins continued for some time, a blot on the conservation record, but the USFWS was trying to exercise the "precautionary principle," acting to protect the cats until sufficient data could be obtained to gauge their status.

THE LEOPARD SURVEY

As noted, when the USFWS listed the leopard as Endangered species in 1973, one effect was to prevent importation of leopard skins into the United States, including legally taken hunting trophies. U.S. hunters were incensed. On January 3, 1978, Safari Club International petitioned the Department of the Interior to propose reclassifying the leopard from Endangered to Threatened. Keith Schreiner, USFWS associate director, called to see if I was interested in conducting a survey of the leopard in Africa south of the Sahara. My credentials were involvement in conservation in Africa as a professor at the University of Pretoria and as project leader for work funded by the grant to Texas A&M University from the Caesar Kleberg Foundation for Wildlife Conservation.

I agreed with the objectives of the project, accepted Keith's proposal, and enlisted Wendell Swank as a partner; between the two of us, we had unusually good contacts in the conservation community in Africa. We were cordially received and data were freely supplied by those we interviewed. Although we knew that field studies would be far more scientific, they were impossible given the scope of the project.

Preparations began in early October 1976. With a letter of introduction from USFWS Director Lynn G. Greenwalt, we made plans to interview executive officers, research scientists, and government and private conservationists throughout southern and East Africa concerning the status of the species in their jurisdictions. We also searched the records and the literature for information about the distribution and abundance of leopards. Except for nations and regions involved in civil wars, we visited most nations south of the Sahara. Thirty-one interviews, in addition to our discussions and research, formed the foundation for our conclusions.

Every person we interviewed who was employed by a conservation agency was of the opinion that the leopard was not currently endangered or threatened with extinction in the relevant country. Considering the knowledge, background, and experience of the interviewees, we believed the information on the status of the leopard was sound. The data cast serious doubt about whether the leopard belonged on CITES Appendix I (Endangered) or should more properly placed on Appendix II (Threatened).

There was virtually no support from the people we interviewed for permitting leopard products to enter the commercial skin trade once more. The ready market and high economic return for skins were most frequently cited as the major causes for the decline in leopard numbers. Destruction of habitat by agricultural activities was also frequently mentioned.

Our conclusion was that placement of the leopard on the list of species classified as Endangered was not defensible. We proposed two alternative positions to the U.S. Department of the Interior. The first was to retain the leopard on Appendix I (Endangered) but to permit importation of trophy skins into the United States by sport hunters. This would require changing U.S. policy and establishing a quota system, like some other governments had. The second alternative was to put the leopard on Appendix II (Threatened) where, like other species that faced a threatening long-term prognosis, it could be managed and conserved and ultimately saved from extinction through wise use.

We recommended the second alternative, and CITES finally agreed that a change in the official status of the species was warranted. The leopard was downlisted to Threatened. Although we did not presume that our report was responsible for changing the regulations for importing leopard products into the United States, we believed that it impacted the decision. CITES provided quotas for the taking of leopards, where they were requested and where the numbers of animals were known to be sustainable in managed populations. The United States, however, has not honored these quotas.

Before describing the somewhat different trajectory of our later jaguar study, and before leaving matters African, I should recount two asides from South Africa's neighboring country of Namibia, which I visited during the leopard survey.

ATTILA THE HUN

The cultural mores of people around the world are important to conservation. Most conservationists soon learn that problems in conservation are largely people problems, and solutions must reflect the socio-economic context of the people affected. I learned this over and over working abroad and at home. The following account of German rancher's encounter with a leopard in Namibia serves as an admittedly extreme example.

Southwest Africa, renamed Namibia at its independence in the late 1960s, was a German colony until the end of World War I, when it was made a Protectorate of South Africa by the League of Nations. A vast, sparsely populated nation, it consisted primarily of desert and semiarid land with little surface water but abundant wildlife. Livestock was its major agricultural commodity. Many Southwest Africans fought for Germany in both world wars. Even today, the German language is prominent in Namibia.

After the German defeat in World War I, a rancher named Attila Port returned to Namibia but never acknowledged the defeat of his motherland. He continued to wear his uniform and carried his arms wherever he went. He remained a German soldier until the end, a stereotype of unreconstructed German culture and values, which he expressed in severe ways to his family and everyone else. Life was hard for Attila and his family. Ranching was their livelihood; wildlife was a major source of meat; water was always scarce; and large lands were required to keep enough cattle to support a family. Predators had no currency in this context. Thousands were killed to protect livestock and game. Some areas were stripped entirely of large cats, hunting dogs, and other carnivores.

Practically everyone in Southwest Africa knew Port by reputation and had heard his story and seen him in his uniform with the peaked hat that identified German soldiers. His son, also named Attila, was born into this setting and was expected to engage in whatever pursuits provided for the family. Attila cropped antelope for meat and other products, which were shipped to Germany and other southern European countries. He became a game cropper in tsetse fly control efforts in Southern Rhodesia (now Zimbabwe) and Northern Rhodesia (now Zambia), where he killed antelope, warthogs, buffalo, and other large mammals that were primary hosts to the flies. The flies in turn were primary hosts to a protozoan that carried the disease trypanosomiasis or sleeping sickness, a dreaded disease afflicting livestock and people over much of Africa south of the Sahara.

I met the junior Attila while in Namibia to conduct interviews about the status of leopards, and he was eager to tell his story of a fight with a leopard. Incredulous at first, I found myself becoming enthralled as his story unfolded. It was as if he had fully re-engaged with the leopard while telling the story. I include it for the light it casts upon the practices of people in remote and harsh environments. What he told me was astounding, but I did not question the truth of his account. Dr. Eugene Joubert, the director of research in government conservation agency and later the mayor of Windhoek, the capital city, was with me and did not show disbelief. Here is what Port told us in his somewhat fractured English:

My father, when he finished the Hottentot War during the settlement years, he went out for farming. He went with few cattle, sheep, and goats. So the leopards caught lots of these—some of the stock. They had to protect the stock. We're six children, and my father sent us to very, very good schools to get us a good education. To have six children in school, you must protect your stock. So my father killed the leopards. He killed 269 from 1907 until 1961. So then I was brought up by my father to kill the leopards.

Later, when I couldn't stand it (killing the leopards), let's do the other way now. There is another way, and I was the first person in Southwest to do it—to catch them alive in cage traps. I built especially a cage trap to catch these animals—cage trap. I caught in a few years 111 leopards alive and let them free, some in Ethosha Park, some in Kruger Park and the rest in zoos in the United States, Japan, Manila and all over the world in parks.

As I said before, we are six children. I had five sisters and I am the only son. My father was one of the highest decorated officers in the German Army. He got the best medals for bravery you can have now. One son between five sisters can only be a sissy. He brought me up very, very hard.

One day we had visitors from Europe—trophy hunters. They had film cameras and still cameras. We went to the place I had set a trap for a leopard. My father always said you must give a chance to the leopard. Don't turn the trap up and then go in and just shoot. Give him a chance; let him go away. So you must follow up, and if you are not strong enough, the leopard has the right to kill you. We'll never be prepared to help you.

That day he gave me only one round of ammunition and I always had my bayonet. When I was taught by my father to kill the leopard, I was only allowed to kill them with my bayonet when they charged. Then you have to kill him. I was not allowed to shoot him. That day he took my bayonet off, and he said I will give you one round of ammunition. Today you must show if you are a man or not. Nobody is allowed to help you. Even the trophy hunters from Europe put their rifles away. He said afterwards you can shoot the leopard, but today I will show you something. If the leopard kills me, he has the right to kill me.

I had to walk—they were behind me—up to thirty meters from the leopard. They took some shots with their cameras. My father said I must walk closer and if he jumps out, I must keep him, with the rifle, down so they can take action photos. Nobody is allowed to help me, and I am not allowed to shoot. The trophy hunters must afterwards shoot the leopard.

I walked closer and I said to my father, Can I run? If the leopard jumps out I will run. I don't like that the leopard must kill me today. He said, if you turn and run away, it's no accident, I'll shoot you, definitely. So my only way was to go straight into the leopard, and he jumped out. The first, he touched the ground, and the second he was right on me with such a force I fell down. The leopard was on top of me and we started fighting. I was on top and the leopard was down and then he was on top. I was terribly bitten and scratched by that leopard.

For awhile, I had a blackout. I thought: better now you get moving. I put my feet under the leopard's body and I kicked him away several meters. Before I was up, he was on me again and was on top of me. I heard my mother screaming. My mother was with me; my two sisters were there too. They came and they said, 'Attila, we'll help you.' So I heard my father chase them away. Today you'll see the strongest will survive.

I had a second blackout and now every power I got my feet under his body and gave him a hell of a kick this time. But before he was up—I wasn't allowed to load the rifle so I had to get a round in before the leopard charged again on me—I shot his head to pieces. Really until today, I don't know how it happened. Up to the moment when the leopard had me down, and we were fighting, I was terribly scratched and bitten all over. I didn't feel a sore place—nothing. It is a wonderful time to die if you have to die. You don't feel anything.

So then I had a blackout and when I came to, I was in the bath in the farmhouse. There was luckily a medical doctor, but he had no narcotics with him. I saw him with the scissors cutting away all the loose flesh and skin where I was scratched and bitten. He cut it open and I saw I was just sitting in blood in the bath and he was cleaning and washing me. So I had another failure for a long time. When I was in my bed, then the pain started but not before.

I told him it was an amazing story and I supposed he had been lucky. "Yes, I was," Port replied. "I was brought up this way. My father said if you want to live, you must look after yourself. Nobody must help you!" Even if the story is not true, it offers some indications about people meeting the challenges of their environment and about circumstances to be considered in conservation plans.

THE CHEETAH IN NAMIBIA

Unlike the adaptable leopard, which flourishes in a wide range of habitat types from mountains to savanna and dense riverine forest, the cheetah is a creature of open country. In the mid-1970s, Norman Myers estimated that the world population was some one hundred thousand cheetahs. Loss of habitat to agriculture and other human activities was the primary factor in the declining numbers and distribution of the species. East and southern Africa still contain sizable populations, but cheetahs are now believed to be absent from the Middle East, where they were once abundant. They were used in the Arab countries as coursers for hunting game and were reared in captivity for that purpose.

Now extirpated from many African countries, cheetahs have maintained their numbers and even increased in Namibia. Censusing the species is difficult because cheetahs have large home ranges and move over wide areas of country. But recent estimates by the Cheetah Conservation Fund indicate that the number in Namibia is some four thousand animals, up from about twenty-five hundred as recently as the mid-1980s.

Hunting cheetahs is legal in Namibia, and safari hunting is big business. More than 95 percent of the suitable habitat is privately owned. The country also contains several large reserves, among them the famous Etosha Pan. Cheetah habitat has been maintained largely because the semiarid climate is better suited to livestock operations, game farming, and hunting than to intensive agriculture. Large ranches and low human numbers have meant that Namibia has some of the best remaining cheetah habitat.

From earliest settlement times, cheetahs were considered vermin and were relentlessly controlled by landowners. They are easily captured because they habitually mark prominent trees with urine and feces to advertise that they have been or are in the area. The selected trees usually have angled branches onto which the cheetah can climb to view the surroundings. Ranchers have used poison, rifles, and even aircraft to kill cheetahs, but most are trapped at the trees. Cheetahs travel as family groups—females with cubs—or as lone males. When one member of a

"Play trees" are important in cheetah ecology. A cheetah communicates its presence in a region by depositing fecal material and urine on play trees. These are somewhat larger than other trees in the area and usually have limbs that lean away from the trunk. Cheetahs climb and rest on these leaning limbs. Ranchers soon learn which trees the animals use and set walk-in traps there for them. Often a single set may catch several, up to five in a family group.

family group is caught in a box trap, it is placed in a compartment in the back of the trap as enticement for other family members to enter. Many are killed in the traps. Few places exist where they can be shipped for release.

Cheetahs travel over great areas. Typically, they may be seen frequently on a ranch for a few days and then not seen again on the same ranch for months. They are not readily baited to a carcass, as are leopards and lions, because cheetahs generally take only live prey and eat fresh meat. They seldom revisit a carcass more than a day or two old. Yet ranchers sometimes succeed in killing them by lacing a fresh kills with poison such as strychnine. Once that has been ingested, few cats survive. Unfortunately, secondary poisoning of nontarget animals frequently occurs as poisons are transferred from carcass to carcass. Trophy hunting—generating income for ranchers, and in the process providing cheetahs some economic traction because of their value to landowners as trophies—seems decidedly preferable to ongoing persecution as vermin.

The Management Plan

Cheetah trophies cannot be imported into the United States because of the spotted cat listing, even though hunters may be issued licenses and export permits by the government of Namibia. Some trophies are in storage in Namibia awaiting the possibility of the U.S. government changing its policy; other countries issue import permits for trophies taken by their citizens, provided the hunters have valid export permits from the country hunted.

The sportsmen's lobbying organization Conservation Force, led by the director, John J. Jackson III, decided to become involved on behalf of several hunters attempting to obtain import permits for cheetahs killed in Namibia. The U.S. government position has been that it will not issue an import permit for any species on Appendix 1 without evidence that the home country has a management plan for the species and that the population benefits from the taking of the animal. Most range states have conservation agencies in their governments, but personnel and financial support are not available to undertake studies of the required magnitude and rigor.

In 1992, Namibia and Zimbabwe petitioned CITES for a quota of cheetahs that could be taken legally. Namibia was granted a quota of 150 animals and Zimbabwe, 50. The quotas included animals for sport hunting and problem animals caught and exported elsewhere. The petition stated that none of the proponents intended to kill cheetahs for their skins and that there would be no cropping or captive breeding of the species for this purpose.

Efforts to ease U.S. restrictions on the importation of these trophies have so far failed despite lawsuits filed by Conservation Force. The United States would not relent on their strict requirements for taking a cheetah. I served on the board of Conservation Force, and I attempted to assist in the effort to relax restrictions, on the basis of managing wildlife to benefit people.

Conservation Force developed a plan to raise funds by charging a management fee to hunters wanting to take cheetah. Meetings were held with Namibia's wildlife agency, professional hunters' association, and several other conservation and hunting organizations. A contract was developed for landowners and Conservation Force to charge a fee of about one thousand dollars per hunter to be set aside for studies of cheetah ecology and management.

Although all parties went on record as favoring the agreement, few hunters participated, and funds were meager. The matter of hunting cheetahs in Namibia and their importation into the United States languishes there.

THE JAGUAR SURVEY

Perhaps because the jaguar is closer to home, or because it once occurred in Arizona and South Texas, the United States stance on the jaguar has been a little different. As in the case of the leopard, hunters and the fur industry challenged the U.S. government's designation of the jaguar as Endangered, claiming that because no surveys of the species' status had been conducted, the requirements for listing had not been met.

The CITES listing was crucial to curbing the skin trade. By the 1980s it was clear that the changes in international law had destroyed the market for pelts, and with no market and falling favor in the fashion industry, poaching all but ended. But American hunters alleged that they had data on the status of cats and that the number of jaguars taken annually by sportsmen was very low. A heated debate developed over the issue.

This time the U.S. Fish and Wildlife Service decided to fund several projects on the jaguar and other cats of interest. Keith Schreiner again contacted me to ask if I would be interested in participating in a survey of the jaguar in Central and South America. Wendell and I developed a survey instrument and began the project in 1986, dividing up between us the nations we were to visit on three trips to Latin America.

The project was exceptionally interesting. We learned a lot about conservation in those nations and came to appreciate the valiant efforts being made to protect resources and use them wisely. We also learned about the difficulties in managing wildlife without proper funding or experienced field biologists and, in some cases, with rampant chicanery and mischief by politicians.

Over the course of several weeks, we visited twenty-two nations in Central and South America, where we interviewed fifty-six organizations and individuals. Interviews were tape-recorded and transcribed at the end of the day. Copies of the interviews were returned to the interviewees for their review to make sure we had recorded their comments correctly. Most people we interviewed were professionals employed with conservation agencies and non-government organizations. Some were conducting research on cats at the time of our visit. Others were administrators of state or national wildlife agencies.

With this information, we estimated the numbers of jaguars and mapped their distribution in each country. We then developed a combined map showing distribution and comparative numbers, and we filed a 361-page final report presenting our conclusions and recommendations.

We concluded that under existing conditions of administration and management of wildlife resources, the jaguar should be retained on Appendix I of the Convention on Trade in Endangered and Threatened Species (CITES). We found no enthusiasm on the part of wildlife organizations or scientist-conservationists for changing its status—that is, for taking it off the protected list and permitting hunting—and we did not recommend a change of status.

Loss of habitat will continue, and this factor will likely deliver a telling blow to the species' persistence and survival in much of its present range. Attitudes among rural people are utilitarian, and the idea of preserving wildlife for its own sake or for the future is not a strong force. It is also obvious that ranchers will continue to protect their livestock from predation by wild animals. Only a few larger ranches have the capability to protect the species as an object of sport hunting, which is presently illegal in practically all countries in Latin America.

We suggested that some measures should be instituted to make the jaguar a positive rather than a negative force. We noted that should sound management be instituted in selected areas of the jaguar's range, we viewed wise use of the species through sport hunting as a positive measure for protecting it in the long term. Given some economic worth through hunting-derived revenue, viable populations of the species can likely be protected in parks and reserves, which are presently its chief remaining bastions of protection in certain countries.

We further concluded that periodic evaluations of jaguar populations should be initiated in areas where the species has maintained its numbers and is presently a factor in livestock management. Little organizational or financial support can be expected from in-country sources. Rather, a cooperative effort by administrative agencies and donor conservation organizations will likely be necessary to develop more systematic management.

Following the filing of our report, the Venezuelan government approached Wendell and me to develop a management plan, including hunting, in a region where jaguar predation on livestock was a serious problem. We developed the plan with careful attention to taking only problem animals. The proposal was not accepted. The Audubon Society of Venezuela campaigned against hunting jaguars in the country, and several hunting clubs objected to allowing outside visitors to hunt jaguars. Apparently, Venezuelan hunters wanted no competition. At the time, I served on the board of the National Audubon Society in North America, but the issue had not surfaced in U.S. Audubon circles. As the Venezuelan government had requested the management plan, we had not anticipated objection to hunting jaguars. The obvious lesson from this experience is to make sure that all interests are invited to the table when plans and decisions are made.

FURTHER READING

Teer, James G., and Wendell G. Swank. *Status of the Leopard in Africa South of the Sahara*. A Report to the Office of Endangered Species. Washington, D.C.: U.S. Fish and Wildlife Service, 1977. 264 pages.

Teer, James G., and Wendell G. Swank. *Status of the Jaguar in Latin America*. Washington, D.C.: National Fish and Wildlife Foundation, 1987. 361 pages.

CHAPTER TEN

The Saiga Antelope

SOME WILDLIFE species have commercial value, and this puts them at risk of poaching and over-exploitation if they are valued for products available only at their death. Poaching is a problem wherever people are hungry and where commercial gain has brought wildlife to the marketplace.

Effects of poaching and overuse of species for their utilitarian products are exceeded only by loss and degradation of habitat. A great many cultures and indigenous peoples have long depended on bush meat and used animals for their skins and as sources of medicines, ornaments, and totems. Such traditional use obviously depends on maintaining the wildlife and rarely threatens the survival of species. But when species are harvested for commerce, the pressure can easily become too great for them to maintain their numbers. Recreational hunting is a favored modern use of wildlife, and wildlife management as we know it in North America arose partly to constrain the ravages of over-exploitation and commerce so as to ensure that species of interest to hunters would persist. The lists of endangered and threatened species kept by various conservation organizations are telling barometers. In a nutshell, these lists show hundreds of candidates for listing as endangered and threatened, and the lists have grown longer and longer. However, there simply are not enough funds available even for full review of all those listed or proposed for listing, let alone for their effective management. Few species have been removed from the lists as a result of successful management actions.

Although I understand that recreational hunting and game cropping are out of favor today in many countries, it still seems to me that the old phrase "use it or lose it" has a place in management of some species.

Only in the last the last few decades has the conservation fraternity had formal programs to protect and rescue wildlife at risk, and these remain fragile. The U.S. Endangered Species Act has had a tortured history; Congress has been reluctant to renew it. By contrast, humanity has had a long history of coexisting with wildlife while using it.

The saiga antelope (*Saiga tatarica*) in the semiarid and steppe habitats of Eurasia was an abundant species and was managed and used for centuries by the Russians for both its meat and its horns. It has a long history as a commercially valuable species in these dry lands: concoctions made from its horns are presumed to have medicinal values highly prized by Orientals and some Russians. This practical value has served as motivation to preserve the saiga's precarious existence.

Now, it is threatened with extirpation from its range around the Caspian Sea. Destruction of its habitat through over-grazing and over-exploitation of the declining herds are recognized as the two factors responsible for its status. The Autonomous Republic of Kalmykia, a member of the Russian Federation (CIS), contains the bulk of the population in the region. In the mid-1990s the saiga was accepted by CITES as an Appendix II (Threatened) species. Because it has value to several countries around the Caspian Sea, and there is reason to believe the population can recover, it has not been accepted for Appendix I (Endangered) listing.

I first became aware of the saiga antelope while studying for my B.S. degree at Texas A&M University. Dr. William B. Davis, an eminent mammalogist and head of the Department of Wildlife and Fisheries Sciences, taught mammalogy. His lecture on the large mammals of the world was responsible for my interest in them. There were no recent publications about the species. Information was not available during World War II or the Cold War. Visas to visit Russia for scientific purposes were practically impossible to obtain.

In 1961, the Russians published the excellent monograph *Biology of the Saiga*, by A. G. Bannikov, L. V. Zhirnov, L. S. Lebedev, and A. A. Fandeev. It became available to the world through the Israeli Translation Service in 1967 and was among the first scientific books translated by the Israelis. At the end of the Cold War, the book became the primary source of information on the species, the benchmark and engine for promoting research and management of the saiga.

By the 1980s, the saiga had suffered a precipitous decline. Through the U.S. Department of State, the Russians requested assistance from the U.S. Fish and Wildlife Service to assist in developing management plans to curb the decline. USFWS Director Bob Jantzen asked me to work on a project with several Russian scientists in Kalmykia. My work for the

USFWS Office of International Affairs on several projects in India surely helped in my selection. I was delighted at the prospect of working with saiga in their native range.

My first visit to Russia and Kalmykia was in 1991, when the Soviet Union was dissolving. There was some degree of unrest and civil disobedience, and commerce had stalled. That was when President Boris Yeltsin stood atop the tank and defied the old guard in their efforts to retain power. The upheaval did not affect us except that food was not plentiful or easily obtained, even in remote villages. Boiled eggs, borsch (beet and cabbage soup) and dark bread were about the only fare in cafés.

During this visit I was introduced to Valeri Neronov in Moscow. Valeri was deputy director of the Man and the Biosphere program for Russia. He was a well-traveled conservationist known for his work on mammals in Mongolia. His assistant, Anna Luchenkova, was knowledgeable about conservation of the saiga. I was always accompanied by Valeri and on some visits by both Valeri and Anna. They were essential to the project because I was not fluent in Russian but they were fluent in English.

On my second visit to Moscow I was startled to learn that Lir Zhirnov, one of the four authors of the saiga monograph, was a colleague of Valeri's and was still engaged in studies of saiga ecology and management. By most counts, he should have been deceased. A kindly gentleman, Lir was indeed a valuable source of information. He accompanied me to the field on two occasions. I gave him an English edition of his book. He had not seen an English copy, and it pleased him to receive it and me to present it.

We traveled by Aeroflot to Elista, the capital of Kalmykia, and spent the next seven days visiting the steppes and the saiga, which were on their annual migration to their lambing grounds. From such vantage points as there were in the flat and slightly undulating terrain, we were in the midst of the saiga herd as we began contemplating the potential for management. Officials of the government of Kalmykia and the federal government of Russia were cordial and as helpful as their resources allowed.

From Elista, we traveled by car to Yashkul, a village in the heart of the saiga range. We stayed in the local game warden's camp. He was a veteran of World War II and became friendly despite our inability to communicate. When he learned from Valeri that I too was a veteran of World War II and had served in the U.S. Navy in the Pacific, he invited me to an evening with him and his vodka. He wanted to talk about his experiences as a foot soldier at the siege of Stalingrad, now named Volgograd. I declined that invitation. He was a large bear of a man, and his experiences and capacity for vodka were both far more substantial than mine; and I knew what the outcome of a party might be. Later I did hear his stories through an interpreter. The Russians are still not far from their grief at the ravages of World War II, when they lost 20 million in the course of stopping the Germans.

I was not engaged in continuous field research with the Russians and Kalmykians but worked with and for them whenever I could. Financial support covered my daily expenses and travel between the United States and Russia. As the director of the Rob and Bessie Welder Wildlife Foundation, I asked the trustees for my salary while working on this project, and it was granted. Support came primarily from the U.S. Fish and Wildlife Service, the Welder Foundation, and Conservation Force. Census of the saiga population in Kalmykia was an annual requirement and was expensive. We usually carried funds personally to the Russians in amounts of five thousand dollars. On one occasion, Dr. Fred Lindzey, leader of the Montana Cooperative Wildlife Research Unit, and I each delivered five thousand dollars to the Kalmyks so that an aircraft could be rented for census work.

I also attended international meetings where I met with colleagues on the saiga project to review and plan work. The project was a happy time for me as it included time in the field with interesting people, introduced me to the unique biological system of the desert steppes, and had the potential to contribute to the welfare of a species in trouble. Local people were the core of the project, and I served it by finding funds and making known the plight of this once abundant species. Together we attempted to promote their status and future.

My last trip to Russia was in 2002 to a three-day saiga workshop in Elista organized by the Convention on Migratory Species, an arm of the United Nations Environmental Program. It was well attended by representatives of nations with saiga on their lands. The purpose of the workshop was to determine the animal's status, a prelude to nominating it to Appendix I (Endangered); to date the species remains on Appendix II.

BIOLOGY AND RESEARCH

The saiga is a herd of animals about the size of the American pronghorn antelope. It has interesting morphological and behavioral adaptations for living in arid steppe habitats. Enlarged nasal vestibules containing a dense nexus of blood vessels serve to warm the cold air that the animal breathes and to filter the sand, which is omnipresent and is taken in because of the saiga's habit of running with its nares close to the ground. Saiga are shy, with large flight distances. It is almost impossible to approach them within a few hundred yards. They are alert and run in a mass when approached.

Legs on the same side are moved simultaneously, giving a strange appearance of immobility. A herd seen from afar appears as a level blanket being pulled over the grassland, rising and falling with the terrain.

Occasionally the saiga leaps or bounds to gain height for looking around, always moving fast in a cloud of sand and dust. The orbits of its eyes protrude, an adaptation of animals of open terrain that need wide peripheral vision. Its escape maneuver is to run rather than to seek cover.

Saiga migrate between summer and winter ranges and moves nomadically in response to rainfall and green forage. Concentrations of tens of thousands in the lambing range have made them vulnerable despite extra wardens placed in the region to prevent poaching.

The female reaches sexual maturity at eight months and the male at seven to twelve months. Twins are the norm, an anomaly for a bovid, and gestation is from 135 to 150 days. Only the males have horns, and the mating system is a harem arrangement whereby a single male may collect and keep five to twenty females. These sexual characteristics provide for fecundity and the ability to recover quickly from losses. Saiga have demonstrated this important characteristic when their numbers have been reduced by disease, starvation, and other causes.

CAUSES OF THE PRESENT DECLINE

Most of my time in Russia was spent in the field with Valeri, Anna, and local Kalmykian biologists of government organizations. We had visits with the president of Kalmykia and his minister of the environment as well as with leaders in the agricultural and conservation agencies and university faculties. All were sympathetic to the species' needs and pledged support for it. We kept in close contact with the Department for Conservation, Monitoring and Management for Game Resources for the Republic of Kalmykia, the agency responsible for wildlife conservation and hunting. We also fully informed the Russian Department of Protection and Development of Hunting Resources, within the Ministry of Agriculture, about activities of the saiga project in Kalmykia.

In addition, Valeri and his colleagues in neighboring nations organized colloquia and workshops on the biology and management of the species. I authored and published several papers presenting information on the saiga to expand awareness of its difficulties. Historically, disease, severe weather, human intervention on the species' range, and predation by wolves have all been factors that at one time or another have been responsible for enormous losses of saiga, but the population has usually bounced back. During the time of our project, however, the saiga population was steadily falling, eventually to numbers from which we feared it could not recover.

Grazing is the primary industry of the Kalmykians. Formerly nomadic grazers from Mongolia, they have grazed sheep in herding systems for centuries. About four hundred years ago, the Kalmykians entered the region in southern Russia alongside the Caspian Sea. They became residents and are now an enclave of Buddhists in the Autonomous Republic of Kalmykia. They continue to practice livestock husbandry, but much of the steppe grassland is now overgrazed. In addition, attempts to farm the grasslands have ended in wind erosion and loss of topsoil.

Of all factors causing the decline of saiga in Kalmykia, overgrazing by livestock, primarily sheep, is the major one. More than 20 percent of the habitat is now degraded to desert with blowing sand and dunes. More than 50,000 acres are lost annually to overgrazing of the fragile environment.

The entire population of Kalmykians, more than three hundred thousand people, were put on trains and sent to Siberia during the aftermath of World War II. The Russians believed they had not fought valiantly against the Germans approaching the Stalingrad regions. The Kalmykians were forced to stay in Siberia until 1957, when they were allowed to return. In the meantime, collective farms increased livestock quotas, and overgrazing became more destructive to the habitat.

Poaching was next in importance in the decline of the saiga. After the dissolution of the Soviet Union, poaching grew rampant as civil authority did not reach into the hinterland. The market for saiga horn was a strong draw. Peasants' average annual income was less than a few saiga horns could bring at the market. Poaching rings were common, and exports to Asian nations were routinely allowed through without inspection. Records of the numbers of horns taken illegally and shipped out are obviously not available.

And the poaching was blatant. Twice while in the field, I witnessed poachers on motorbikes racing to catch up with a herd of saiga. On reaching the animals, the poachers threw chains at the males' feet to entangle them. The riders then jumped onto the struggling saiga, cut its throat, and severed its head. All this was done in plain view of me and the game warden but on the opposite bank of a canal too deep for us to cross in our vehicle. We could only watch and curse. On another occasion, we collected two saiga to screen them for parasites. We worked in the field for most of the day. On returning to the area the next day, we discovered twenty-five males that had been shot during the night and had had their heads removed. The meat was left to vultures.

Human development on the steppe has also been responsible for heavy morality of saiga. A network of hundreds of miles of canals was laid out in saiga habitat in Kalmykia to irrigate croplands with water from the Volga River. Some canals are deep and steep sided, producing barriers the antelope cannot negotiate during migration. Many drown in the herd's blind effort to cross. More then 14,000 of them drowned in a particularly deadly crossing in 1990.

According to my Russian colleagues, in the late 1990s predation by wolves became another major mortality factor. Efforts to control wolf numbers have been ineffective. With this added to the other sources of mortality, the species is ever more at risk, and the population continues to decline.

Over the years for which there are reliable records, several instances have been recorded in which more than half of the population was lost. More than 40 percent perished from hunger in the Caspian lowlands during blizzards in 1949–50. Enteritis, a malady of the digestive tract, is a recurring problem in very cold weather and snow. Pneumonia and upper respiratory disease have been responsible for huge losses. One of the major plunges occurred starting in 1978, when the population fell from

A closer view in a museum display shows the saiga's odd nasal adaptations to a world of cold temperatures and blowing sand. As applies to many species, loss of habitat and over-exploitation of wildlife are themes in the saiga story.

715,000 to some 50,000 in 1987. In Kazakhstan more than 500,000 saiga were lost to pasteurellosis in the 1980s.

As noted, the species has traditionally been able to recover quite rapidly due to its fecundity. Nonetheless, years are required for recovery, and when several major morality factors combine in a few short years, the recovery may require decades. I believe the saiga population has reached a state from which it may never recover to its former numbers. Correspondence from Valeri Neronov in 2005 indicated only 20,000 to 30,000 reported in the Blacklands and Caspian lowlands in Kalmykia.

The plight of the species is a nagging problem to the Russians and to the conservation community at large. The Russians and Kalmyks are aware of the problems and needs of the species, but they are strapped for funds and personnel to manage the situation. The 2002 workshop mentioned did offer a dim ray of hope when Concordance was achieved at the workshop, and nations with saiga were asked to join together in a consortium to promote survival of the species. But management planning can only be useful with implementation; I fear the impulse may not reach the field and may remain in a sort of limbo.

The story of the saiga antelope in Russia mirrors that of many species in other parts of the world. The names change but the problems are identical. As a living renewable resource with economic value, the saiga demonstrates the difficulty of management and use of a migratory species in fragile desert and grassland habitats. It is a unique species now worn away by human pressures. Its history is the story of a biological system subject to competing human values and activities. Loss of habitat and over-exploitation of life are common factors afflicting the natural world, and we could not stem the losses that have brought this species to its knees. Management problems are expressed as biological crises; and attempts at solutions reveal that dimensions of the human condition are at stake.

FURTHER READING

Teer, James G. Conservation Status of the Saiga Antelope in Kalmykia and Kazakhstan. Species No.17. Pages 35–38 in *Red Data Book*, Gland, Switzerland: International Union for the Conservation of Nature and Natural Resources (World Conservation Union), 1991.

Teer, J. G., V. M. Neronov, L. V. Zhirnov, and A. I. Blizniuk. 1996. Status and Exploitation of the Saiga Antelope in Kalmykia. Pages 75–87 in *The Exploitation of Mammal Populations*, ed. V. J. Taylor and Nigel Dunstone. London: Chapman and Hall, 1996. 415 pages.

CHAPTER ELEVEN

A Celebration of Continuance

FERDINAND ROEMER, acclaimed as the "father of Texas geology" and a keen observer and recorder of other elements of the natural world in Texas, traveled in July 1846 to Torrey's Trading Post on the upper reaches of the Brazos River to observe the country and its inhabitants. After a short sojourn there, he traveled to Austin and en route traversed the cross timbers, blackland prairies, and Edwards Plateau. He crossed several rivers, including the Brazos, Little River, San Gabriel, and Willis Creek. He encamped for a night at Willis Creek in Williamson County in an area not far from what came to be my family's farm. He wrote in his journal, "After a ride of several days, we came to a little brook called Willes Creek where buffaloes in great numbers were grazing. They covered the grassy prairie separated into small groups and far distant on the horizon, they were visible as black specks. The number of those seen must have been not less than a thousand."

One hundred years later, as a young man in college, I saw those buffalo. They were bones in an Indian kitchen midden. They were there along with the bones of prairie chickens, white-tailed deer, pronghorn antelope, turkeys, herons and other species I did not recognize.

A few months after his stop at Willis Creek, Roemer traveled from San Antonio to an outpost called San Saba in Lipan Apache territory. He camped for the night on the bank of the Llano River and recorded that "Jim Shaw, our Indian companion, bagged a deer and a turkey and Mr. Neighbors caught a number of catfish (*Pimelodus*) each a foot long or more."

While working as a biologist for the Texas Game, Fish and Oyster

Commission and living on the bank of the Llano River, I became acquainted with the descendants of these same white-tailed deer and Rio Grande turkey and catfish. Many generations later, we could see what Roemer and his party ate that night on the Llano. Canyon wrens, Inca doves, rock squirrels, javelinas, blue-winged teal and collared lizards are still there in their native habitats too. The Llano River still flows blue-green, and the mesquites awake in the spring with lime green leaves that change to dark green as spring wanes and the hot summer sets in. Now I like to see the animals and their world as often as I can, because they give me joy and pique my curiosity.

Some animals are gone from this place or that and some from everywhere. Those that are gone, those we now know only from natural history, are mourned by conservationists in a litany of life we have lost. But I submit that "lost without cause" is not an accurate description of their passing. Their going was not without effect. They have created a cause, and their loss serves us in signposting our intemperance with the land and our lives.

Most species remain, some more numerous than before. Beyond the small changes wrought through evolutionary time, they are the same. There is a continuance of life in the natural world. It is the same with people.

As an undergraduate in attendance at a great conference, I saw Aldo Leopold several times in a crowded room. Awed by his place in conservation affairs, and seeing him always surrounded by important-looking men, I did not approach him more closely. I did not meet Leopold there and was never to see him again. He left us soon afterward.

But I know him. I know him from his essays, his humanity, his science, and from others who knew his private as well as his public life. I became a student of one of his students, Bob McCabe, at his university. I occupied a graduate student carrel at 424 University Farm Place, which was his office and a revered symbol of Leopold and his work. Long after his death, students are still inspired by his life and work.

I knew Paul Errington, at least as much as he would let us know him. Every morning, day after day, no matter what the weather, I saw him leaving his office in the old insectory building at Iowa State University, always in hip boots, to go to his marshes and muskrats. We took no courses from him then; he offered none. We misinterpreted his shyness for aloofness. Only in later years did we come to see the inner workings of this man and his science and value his example of dedication and tenacity. Follow the evolution of his writings, and you discover the greening of a lifetime of study.

I knew Clarence Cottam. An irrepressible, positive spirit, he was the conscience to government, to society, and to the conservation community. He had a gift—what a gift—for debate and for rescuing people from their failures and foibles. He once rescued me at a Cooperative Wildlife Research Unit review after a particularly poor presentation of my research on blue-winged teal migration. I was almost too ashamed to show myself when Cottam came to me and told me I had the best information available on blue-winged teal migration in western Iowa, and that the information would have far-reaching effects in management of the Central Flyway. He knew, and I knew, what he was doing. The human spirit needs men like Clarence Cottam.

And I knew Ira Gabrielson, not well but well enough to recognize his force. A great hulking figure of a man, he was a presence wherever he went. He turned a $75,000 grant request to a private foundation into an award of $1.2 million simply by speaking for an idea and supporting the people who had made the request.

And I knew Bob McCabe, George Burger, Al Hochbaum, Gus Swanson, Dan Leedy, Durward Allen, Joe Hickey, W. B. Davis, and Larry Jahn—all of us brothers. Without question, the most satisfying rewards of my career have been the men and women whom I have known as colleagues and friends. I rejoice at remembering our times together, a lifetime of memories just beneath the surface of my consciousness, beckoned as easily as switching on a light. We are what others have been and what others after us will be. We are the continuance, conservationists all. It is the thread passed through all of the natural world and those who tend it. It makes the human condition acceptable. It is a celebration.

Most of my friends and colleagues have ended their journey, but I prefer to suppose we will gather again. I expect the scene will be familiar. There will be a great mesquite fire. Moving upwind to escape the smoke, the men will hover around the fire in a competition to stay warm. Some will burn aluminum beer cans in the hot fire. Our dogs will be tied nearby. Coyotes will be close and their yipping and howls will resonate through hills and canyons.

At daylight, quail will break their covey ring and wait for the dew to dry before they move. Deer, stamping their front feet and snorting, will carefully venture close to the camp to see what it is all about. The men will break ice on the horse trough and wash their faces, hurrying to get it over with. There will be laughter, teasing, ribald stories, hot coffee, and W. A. Isbell's famous breakfast of a piece of bread on a stick.

We will have reached Llano again.

INDEX

Page numbers in *italics* denote illustrations.

Biology of the Saiga (Bannikov, Zhirnov, Lebedev, & Fandeev), 134

Black Gap Wildlife Management Area, 36

Blankenship, David R., 93

Blankenship, Lytle H., 106

Blocker, John, 65, 115

boats, homemade, 6–7

bobwhite quail, 44, 78, 94–95

Boone and Crockett Club, 69

Bothma, Jacobus du P. (Koos), 33–35

Brothers, Al, 76

Brown, Robert, 68

budgets, conservation, 73

Burger, George V., 59, 60–61, 143, *following p. 18*

Caesar Kleberg Chair of Wildlife Ecology and Management, 40–41, 91

Caesar Kleberg Foundation in Wildlife Conservation (CKFWC), 90, 91, 96, 97

Caesar Kleberg grant to Texas A&M University, 89–91, 105

Caesar Kleberg Research Program in Wildlife Ecology and Management, 91

Caesar Kleberg Wildlife Research Institute, 43

Camargue horses, 95, 96, *following p. 18*

campsites, Apache Ranch, 59–60

The Canvasback on a Prairie Marsh (Hochbaum), 25

cape buffalo, *106*

captive breeding: of deer, 67–69, 76; of nonnative species, 100, *101*

career, vii, 27; academic career, 29–31, 35–37, 40–41, 42; childhood career options, 3, 6; consulting work, 42–45; director of Welder Wildlife Foundation, vii, 27, 38, 41–42; nonnative species research, 90–91, 98–99, 102–104. *See also* international conservation work; research

career choice, wildlife science as, 28–29

Carlander, Kenneth D., 23

Carlisle, John M., 51, 52, 78

catfish "noodling," 48–49

cats. *See* great cats

cattle ranches, consulting work on, 42–45

census methods, 36–37, 43–44

Center for Wildlife Management, South Africa, 35

Central American great cats, 120, 121–22, 130–32

Chaparrosa Ranch, 65

cheetah, 121, 127–30

CITES. *See* Convention on International Trade in Endangered Species of Flora and Fauna

CKFWC. *See* Caesar Kleberg Foundation in Wildlife Conservation

cloning of deer, 76

colleagues, 142–43

commercialization of hunting, 74–75, 97, 100–101. *See also* game ranching

conservation: Asimov on, 71–72; as career choice, 28–29; changing attitudes toward, 31; funding for, 66, 73, 98; hunting and, 66, 133–34; leaders in, viii, 142–43; necessity for, 12–13, 71–72; non-government organizations in, 73

conservation budgets, 73

Conservation Force, 129, 136

conservationist colleagues, 142–43

consulting work, 42–45

Convention on International Trade in Endangered Species of Flora and Fauna (CITES): cheetah, 129; jaguar, 130, 131; leopard, 123; saiga antelope, 134; spotted cat protection, 120, 122

Cook Inlet, 20

Coolidge, Harold J., 55

Cottam, Clarence, 41, 143

cottontail research, 37

Crist, Della, 51, 53

Crist, George, 47, 51–53

grants, research, 37
great cats: Attila the Hun story, 124–27; cheetah, 121, 127–30; jaguar, 120, 121–22, 130–32; leopard, 120, 121, 122–24; protection status, 120–22; trophy hunting of, 121, 123, 129–30; in United States, 121
Greenwalt, Lynn G., 122
Grinnell, George Bird, 53
Guam, 10, 15–16
Gus Engeling Wildlife Management Area. *See* Engeling Wildlife Management Area

habitat degradation, 97, 103–104, 133, 138
habitat protection, oil field activities and, 44–45
Hall, A. S., 46–49, *48*
Harris, Halbert, 22
harvest season, 5–6
Hendrickson, George O., 23, 62
heroes, 53–58
Hewitt, Ollie, 34
Hickey, Joe, 143
Hochbaum, H. Albert, 25, 26, 27, 143
Hodgdon, Harry, 38
Hoffman, Lukus, 96
horse racing, 88, 94, 95
Hoxie House, 13–14
human dimensions of wildlife science, viii–ix, 33, 38–39, 124
human population distribution, in United States, 73
human population growth, 72–73
hunting: in Africa, 114–18; beneficial aspects of, 66, 133; as business entertainment, 43, 115; childhood experiences, 4, 7–9; commercial sport hunting, 67–69, 74–75; fair chase and, 67–69; on King ranch, 94–95; of nonnative species, 95, 97; public criticism of, 66–67. *See also* big game hunting

hunting companions, 58–66
Hutchins, Ross, 79

impala, *107*
international conservation issues, vii, 54–56, 90
international conservation work. *See* Africa; great cats; saiga antelope
international employment opportunities, 40
International Union for the Conservation of Nature (IUCN), 55, 56, 97
introduced species. *See* nonnative species
Iowa State University, 22–23
Isbell, Walter (W.A.), 59, 61–62, *following p. 18*
itinerant workers, 5–6
IUCN. *See* International Union for the Conservation of Nature

Jackson, A. S., 78
Jackson, John J. III, 129
jaguar, 120, 121–22, 130–32
Jahn, Larry, 143
Jantzen, Bob, 134
Jenkins, Jim, 34
Johnson, Belton Kleberg (B. K.), 65
Johnson, Lyndon, B., 105
Jones Foundation, 42

Kalahari Desert safari, 118–19
Kalmykia, 134–36, 138
Kenedy, Mifflin, 88
Kiel, William H. (Bill), 90, 93, 94
King, Captain, 88
King Ranch: Caesar Kleberg Foundation in Wildlife Conservation, 90, 91, 96, 97; Caesar Kleberg grant to Texas A&M University, 89–91, 105; history of, 88–89; horse racing and, 88, 94, 95; hunting on, 88, 89, 94–95; nilgai antelope on, 99, 102–104; nonnative species on, 96–98, 99; Robert J.